POWERHOUSES OF

OHIO

HIGH SCHOOL
FOOTBALL

POWERHOUSES OF

OHIO

HIGH SCHOOL
FOOTBALL

THE '50s AND '60s

TIM RAAB

Foreword by **BOBBY CARPENTER**

THE
History
PRESS

Published by The History Press
Charleston, SC
www.historypress.com

First published 2019

Manufactured in the United States

ISBN 9781467142328

Library of Congress Control Number: 2019937035

In memory of
Antony "Tony" Raab
1973–2007

CONTENTS

FOREWORD

Growing up in Lancaster, Ohio, football has always provided a rite of passage for boys to transition into young men. While many people debate all the things football isn't and all the dangers it can cause young people, there are still so many important lessons that only it can teach.

My father has been a high school football coach for the better part of thirty years. Since starting his coaching career at New Lexington, a small rural Ohio community tucked south of I-70 and east of State Route 33, he has personally witnessed the changes in society and how they have affected the development of young men. Football has become the last bastion of rugged physicality, teamwork and sacrifice for the common good to help develop our nation's young men. Long gone are the days of the military draft and morning Phys Ed calisthenics. Those now belong to yesterday.

But it is yesterday that our nation must never forget. It is our history that defines us as a nation, as a state and as a community. Much of that community history was written through the gridiron. The identity of many of the communities throughout the state once resided in their industry and their football programs. The successes of both seemed so intertwined that they often defined the culture of everyone who lives there.

In my hometown of Lancaster, Ohio, it was no different. Like in much of the state, the factories roared and the football was rough. Those men took pride in their toughness and grit. Whether it was Cleveland, Massillon, Toledo or Steubenville, those tenets remained the same and united entire generations of men throughout the Buckeye State.

Thus, I was honored when Tim Raab asked me to write this foreword to his new book, as it vividly captures what football meant to Ohio towns large and small during a transitional time after World War II and then up to the era of the playoff system in 1972. Tim shares the same sense of the values I do—that football imparts growth lessons on young kids just entering manhood, draws all peoples together for a common cause and creates a unique sense of camaraderie rarely found elsewhere. The book's research is comprehensive, and the descriptions of the players, coaches and games are colorful and exciting. All of this and more is in Tim's book.

Ohio high school football not only changed my life, but it also provided the opportunity for my family to change their entire trajectory of our future. I look forward to sharing the folklorish stories with my sons and one day watching their transition to manhood on Ohio's football fields.

BOBBY CARPENTER
Columbus, Ohio
September 2018

Bobby played high school football for the Golden Gales of Lancaster High School and went to The Ohio State University, where he starred for four years as a linebacker, eventually being drafted in the first round by the Dallas Cowboys of the National Football League. His career spanned playing time with the Cowboys, Lions, Rams, Dolphins and the Patriots. After his NFL retirement, he returned to Ohio State, where he obtained an MBA in finance and strategy from Ohio State's Fisher School of Business, where he also teaches part time at the business school. He hosts a local sports radio show and works with ESPN providing color commentary for college games on the weekends. He writes a blog and prepares regular podcasts, all found by going to bobbycarpenter.com. He lives in central Ohio with his wife and four children.

PREFACE

I n this book I will profile some of the great teams and personalities of Ohio high school football during the 1950s and 1960s. It was a different time and place, and these teams established Ohio as a leader in how the game was played and coached, as well as served as innovators in safety, rules and how the game was administrated. It was a seminal period in Ohio high school football history.

Many of those great teams are still famous in Ohio and some nationally. Some are forgotten, one-hit wonders or no longer in existence. Many of the players and coaches were made equally famous and were catapulted to the major college and professional ranks. By providing the reader a year-by-year snapshot from just two decades of a few teams and personalities of the pre-playoff era, I hope to whet your appetite for more, to get to know the heritage and traditions that make up Ohio high school football and attain an appreciation of how much this sport means to this state.

I made my selections based on each team's success in the decade in which they are described and/or how interesting their stories would appeal to the reader. All records were cross-checked as much as possible using multiple sources, and any errors or omissions are mine alone. Enjoy, and remember: if it hurts, put ice on it and get back in there!

ACKNOWLEDGEMENTS

Putting together a book like this was a dream of mine for many years—but where and how to begin? Certainly, newspapers were excellent sources, and I did go through an awful lot of microfilm in libraries around the state. For those libraries I did not get to in person, I relied on the good graces of the reference librarians in towns large and small. I have to say that I have never met a more cooperative group of people overall than reference librarians. They gave me the type of service on the other end of a phone or an e-mail as if they were just waiting for my call and champing at the bit to begin searching for those little nuggets that prove so valuable to the writer. This personal service was outstanding, and I would like to thank the following as representative of them all for helping me make this book come alive: Rebecca Larson-Troyer, reference librarian, Local History Department, Barberton Public Library; Amanda Dias, reference assistant, Rodman Public Library, Alliance, Ohio; and Ron Davidson, archives librarian, Sandusky Public Library, Sandusky, Ohio. Please support them and your local library!

I also want to mention Carol Copley, senior staff assistant, Sports Information Office, University of Notre Dame, who helped me with information on Augie Bossu.

Standing tall among the school administrators I spoke to was Carol Bebout, the former principal of Marion Harding High School in Marion, Ohio, who over two years gave me much encouragement from our first casual discussion of the project right up to the end, prompting and pushing me to make it happen. Thanks so much, Carol!

Marty Hyland, athletic director of Cleveland Benedictine High School, was tremendous in sharing photos of the 1957 state champs. Likewise for Doug Etgen of Columbus Bishop Watterson and Karen Perone at the Alliance, Ohio Historical Society. Extra special thanks go to Dave Jingo at Canton City Schools for supplying Canton McKinley photos, encouragement and a great helping hand—he is the best. Jan Gluth at the Port Clinton High School Alumni Association and Barb Loudon of the Salem High School Alumni Association were extremely helpful.

Generously supplying photos of both the Fremont Ross Little Giants and the Sandusky Blue Streaks was Vince Guerrieri, author of *The Blue Streaks and Little Giants: More than a Century of Sandusky and Fremont Ross Football* (The History Press, 2013). You can read more about his work at http://vinceguerrieri.com.

In addition, many of those mentioned here introduced me to local historians and fans who have compiled statistics and/or written monographs or short histories of their town's high school football program. Some have published their own books on the subject. Some of these local experts are Jim Kalla (Cincinnati Roger Bacon), Denny Hirsch (Cincinnati Colerain) and Sherry Sheffield (Cincinnati Wyoming).

Marietta High School fans and alumni were some of the most enthusiastic about this project, and I cannot thank them enough!

Tim Hudak owns Sports Heritage Publications in Cleveland and has written some of the best high school football histories ever. Tim gave me some great advice, and his critiques of my writing helped me a lot. He can be found at www.sportsheritagepublications.com.

Deep thanks to Larry Duck of Martins Ferry, Bob Fogle of Marietta and Tony Demarco of Parma.

In this age of networked communications, websites abound that focus on national, state and local high school football. Many webmasters and owners of those sites were kind enough to share data with me and enthusiastically engage on high school football. Their kindness just confirmed that the passion for high school football is greater than any other sport in the country. Some of them include Gary Vogt, the historian for the amazing (and best of them all) Massillon Tiger Football Booster Club's Museum Group, www.massillontigers.com; James Parks and the others at Steubenville's www.rollredroll.com; David Runion from www.fostoria.org; and the gracious and newly married Sara Klein, digital collections coordinator of the excellent Upper Arlington Archive, located at the Upper Arlington Library and reached at http://www.uaarchives.org/index.htm, one of the coolest sites to see the history of a community. And their UA yearbook collection is outstanding! Check it and the rest of them out.

Chris Beaven, the sports editor of the Canton Repository (www.cantonrep.com), was quite generous permitting me to use photos from his organization.

Thanks go to Tim Stried of the Ohio High School Athletic Association for his kind help in answering my many questions. Its website, www.ohsaa.org, is chock full of high school football records and information.

My acquisitions editor, John Rodrigue, was outstanding, his guiding hand throughout the book's construction sure and patient, and the book would not be in your hands if not for him.

Lastly, I want to recognize my football-playing teammates and the Marion Harding class of 1971.

Joy to the world…Joy to you and me…!

OHIO HIGH SCHOOL FOOTBALL

The First Sixty Years

The history of high school football in Ohio, like history everywhere, depends first on word of mouth, the telling and relating of events that happened before they are recorded. Then the events are documented and validated, and then we have a record, or at least the beginnings of a record of what happened. Newspapers around the time football got going wrote romantic, warlike descriptions of the games in the literary prose of the era that, many times, prevents the modern reader from knowing exactly what happened. Sometimes the scores were all but forgotten and the names of the players an afterthought. Many of the earliest clashes and beginnings of rivalries began with club teams, nonsanctioned teams or just a bunch of kids with a lot of adrenaline to get rid of, having either read about the game or maybe having seen one someplace and were willing to knock heads with one another. These early games did exist, but a lot of the facts surrounding them were never recorded in much detail, if at all, and are now lost to historians and fans of the game or are not complete enough to merit them as facts.

During this early period, coaches were sometimes nonexistent, and the eligibility of the players was often overlooked—it just wasn't something one spent time worrying about. Sometimes "ringers" were found—older, more experienced guys who may have been former or even current college players home for a visit and recruited into a local game, maybe with a few dollars being slipped their way. Games that started out as just community fun with ad hoc players soon took on another, more formal personality and a more "semi-serious" tenor. Part-time coaches and officials were found, and the surrounding neighborhoods took a more avid interest in the fast-paced game. In this era, contests were often scheduled by the team manager, most times that position being filled by a student who also arranged the transportation, usually wagons or trains. These games were never truly set until both teams arrived at the field, a surprisingly often event considering the high number of cancellations or just plain no-shows that happened back then, with many being caused by transportation problems or harsh weather and a few from genuine fear. Equipment, such as pads and helmets, was mostly nonexistent, and much blood was spilled, with death from an errant blow a possibility.

Many high schools then would date their first year of real, organized football to when a coach was first hired or assigned, or maybe when they first joined a conference and started playing a planned schedule. The games played before that point have taken on a somewhat semi-mythical status in the communities, and we have sometimes little to draw on aside from old newspaper clippings, diaries or the rare interview obtained for a local history of the town. While that's enough in some cases to authenticate the first games, the newspapers rarely gave much detail about the event, even neglecting such important items as the players' first names. Old-time yearbooks are also suspect, and while intriguing to study, they are not reliable sources for validating facts. So, digging into the earliest years of Ohio high school football is not the easiest task for a historian or writer.

The first of thousands of high school football games in Ohio was played on October 25, 1890, between the oldest public high school in the state, Cleveland's Central High School, and the newest high school, Cleveland's University School, which had been open for about six weeks and which won the game, 20–0. Other schools started teams, not rapidly, but most progressively in northern Ohio, where most of the population was located, and then here and there down in the middle and southern parts of the state. Many schools heard of the game from students who had gone to college in the eastern states, where it had started earlier.

For many years, teams took it on themselves to say they were the champions of the state. This means of self-acclamation, of becoming champion without any polls or playoffs, worked to an extent until other schools across the state called them out and challenged them. For instance, in 1900 Oberlin (5-0-1), Youngstown Rayen (4-1-1) and Cleveland Central (6-0) all claimed to be state champs. This craziness continued until 1947, when polling began.

Schools started programs, and some quickly established themselves as powers. Schools in Fostoria, Youngstown, Massillon, Canton, Sandusky, Cleveland, Toledo, Akron and others up north ran up wins and established heated rivalries. Down in central and southern Ohio, schools started programs and slowly built reputations. Columbus-area schools, around the state capital with a large population, began playing in the 1890s and gained some notoriety, as did Cincinnati schools. Smaller schools like Mogadore, Barberton, Piqua, Oberlin, Steubenville, Fremont, New Philadelphia, Dover and Troy also tasted success throughout the first half of the twentieth century. Parochial schools with all-male student bodies and the ability to recruit players were able to build winning records and legacies.

The flu epidemic and World War I put a crimp in the sport during the late 1910s, as did the Great Depression and World War II later in the '30s and '40s. But these events and countless other smaller ones did not impair the desire for young boys to test themselves on the gridiron. In fact, the return of veterans and the growth of businesses in the state after World War II created a new prosperity and general health in the state, where high school athletics and especially football started an accession that would not level off for many decades.

A great example of this resiliency during difficult times is Coach Paul Brown, who spent nine years as the Massillon Washington High School football coach and posted an 80-8-2 record, for a winning percentage of 90.9. His teams won six straight state titles by local acclamation and were acclaimed national champs four times. From a coaching perspective, his time there was a history of firsts. As a booster club innovator, he helped start one in Massillon that was a model for all that followed; he engaged George (Red) Bird to develop the Massillon Tiger Swing Band and created "the greatest show in high school football"; he developed a playbook and scripted plays to be used in the first series against specific opponents; he invented the draw play; he created specific position coaches and demanded year-round coaching commitments; he used the 40-yard dash as a measurement of a player; he placed coaches in the press box; he was the first to use pass protection and facemasks; he created a live tiger mascot; and he started the grading of a player's game performance. On game days, the downtown area would decorate itself with orange and black bric-a-brac, with flags everywhere, and the schedule for the season was placed on a sign in the middle of town. Strong support for high school teams was pervasive, but seldom was it as total as in Massillon, Ohio, where every male newborn gets a miniature football from the booster club.

In *PB: The Paul Brown Story* by Paul himself, with Jack Clary, the coach is quoted as saying, "We wanted to have the best because we wanted our students to see nothing but the best and be content with nothing less than the best—whether in football or any other area."

Before We Get Started, a Quick Look at Ohio High School Football and Life from 1900 to 1950

1900: Three teams claim the state championship, and all three end up sharing it: Oberlin, Youngstown Rayen and Cleveland Central.

1900: Theodore Roosevelt writes an article for the May issue of *St. Nicholas* magazine titled, "The American Boy," about how the boy can become an "American Man."

1902: Fostoria (8-0-1) is proclaimed state champion.

1903: Kenyon Military Academy in Gambier, Ohio, is acclaimed state champ.

State Title Wins, 1895–1919

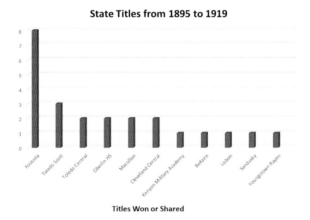

State Titles from 1895 to 1919

Titles Won or Shared

1895	Cleveland Central
1896	Sandusky
1897	none
1898	none
1899	Oberlin High School
1900	Cleveland Central, Youngstown Rayen, Oberlin High School
1901	Rayen, Toledo Central

1902	Fostoria
1903	Kenyon Military Academy
1904	Toledo Central
1905	none
1906	Fostoria
1907	Fostoria
1908	Fostoria
1909	Massillon Washington High School
1910	Fostoria
1911	Fostoria
1912	Fostoria
1913	none
1914	Fostoria, Bellaire High School, Lisbon High School
1915	Fostoria
1916	Toledo Scott, Massillon Washington
1917	none
1918	Toledo Scott
1919	Toledo Scott

1906: The forward pass is legalized, but it takes a few years for it to become widely utilized.

1909: Massillon Washington High School goes 9-0-1, beating Canton McKinley 6–2 at League Park in Canton and completing its best season ever, and is proclaimed state champions.

1910: There are 76 million people in forty-six states.

1912: Fostoria beats Crestline, 131–0; it also scores 596 points in eight games and is named national champion as well as state champ, establishing itself as one of the greatest teams in Ohio schoolboy history.

1914, '16, '17 and '26: Drop-kick field goals are made from 33, 40, 52 and 30 yards away, all still records in Ohio (the last extra point drop-kicked in Ohio was made on October 25, 1913).

1915: Paul Dessenberg of Ashland returns a fumble for a touchdown 102 yards against Mount Vernon.

1916: Toledo Scott is proclaimed state champion along with Massillon Washington and returns to win the title alone in 1918 and 1919. This year (1916), Scott is also proclaimed national champion despite the dispute with Massillon Washington.

1917: The United States enters World War I. No state football champ is proclaimed.

1918: A killer flu pandemic strikes the world hard, killing millions of people before running its course a few years later. Many games were canceled and seasons shortened throughout Ohio.

1918: Toledo Scott beats Stryker, 154–0, Germany surrenders and World War I stops on the eleventh day of the eleventh month at the eleventh hour: November, 11, 1918, at 11:00 a.m.

1919: The American population is 92,407,000 at the end of this decade. Life expectancy for a male is 47.4 years and for a woman 51.8 years.

1920: Canton McKinley and Cleveland East Tech are proclaimed state champions.

1921: No state champion. Cully Berndt of Toledo Waite scores 333 points this season, including fifty-one touchdowns, and Waite scores 666 points in eleven games, fourth all-time in Ohio history. The school averages 60.5 points per game, good for fifth on the all-time list.

1922: Canton McKinley is state champion along with Massillon Washington.

1922: Toledo Waite defeats Cleveland West Tech, 76–0; Doane Academy, 71–0; Louisville Male (Kentucky), 34–0; Harrisburg Tech (Pennsylvania), 52–7; Chicago Lane Tech (Illinois), 66–0; Parkersburg (Virginia), 55–7; Cedar Rapids, Washington (Iowa), 13–2; South Bend (Indiana), 67–6; and Malden (Massachusetts), 18–0, losing only to west side rival Scott, 15–14, on Thanksgiving Day.

1923: Canton McKinley is again state champion, along with East Cleveland Shaw. McKinley goes 19-0 in 1922–23. Warren G. Harding of Marion, Ohio, is president of the United States.

1923: Toledo Scott is proclaimed national champion despite the proclamations made by the McKinley, Cleveland East Shaw and Massillon teams. Scott beat Corvallis, Oregon, 32–0, in 1922 and in 1923 beat Washington High School of Cedar Rapids, Iowa, 24–21, and Columbia Prep of Portland, Oregon, 20–17, to earn the national title.

1923: Erastus "Tunk" Simmons of Medina scores twelve touchdowns in an October 5 game against Spencer. Medina wins that day, 165–0, an Ohio record for most points in a win. Both statistics are simply eye-popping!

1924: Toledo Scott's rival in the Glass City, Toledo Waite, wins the state and national champion crowns by going 10-0, closing with a 46–0 defeat over Boston Everett (Massachusetts).

1926: Bradford goes unbeaten, untied and unscored on, 10-0.

1929–31: Steubenville wins seventeen consecutive shutouts, an Ohio record, and was unbeaten, untied and unscored on in 1930.

1929: There are 106,521,537 people in the United States by the end of the 1920s.

1929: The first night game to be played under the lights in Ohio was held in October in Cleveland, when Cleveland St. Ignatius defeats Cleveland Holy Name, 24–7.

1931: Steubenville gains 734 yards rushing in one game.

1932: Minerva wins ten shutouts.

1932: Toledo Waite finishes a 12-0 season with a 13–7 victory over Miami Senior (Florida) and is invited to the White House.

1932–36: Miamisburg has a thirty-seven-game unbeaten streak (wins and ties).

1935–40: Paul Brown goes 51-1-1 as Massillon Washington's head coach.

1935–36, 1939–40: Massillon Washington is proclaimed national champion.

1937: Massillon Washington High School begins a fifty-two-game unbeaten streak lasting until 1942.

1939: The U.S. population is 123,188,000 by the end of the 1930s; life expectancy is 58.1 for males and 61.6 for females; the average salary is $1,368, and unemployment has risen to 25 percent.

1940: The "jitterbug" becomes the most popular form of dancing, allowing individual expression from each partner.

1941: The empire of Japan launches a surprise attack on Pearl Harbor that brings the United States into World War II.

1941: The penalty flag is first used in a football game, becoming official in 1948; two-platoon football is abolished, and free substitution throughout the game is allowed.

1942: The military and industrial sectors quickly begin to merge together to deliver war goods and, in turn, create millions of jobs for the unemployed.

1943: The sweater look is in for young ladies, and the hairstyle of the time is curls piled up front, with the back reaching down to the shoulders; makeup is in for all women.

1940–45: Films with a story focus of defending our country, sacrifice, the homefront and heroism are commonplace at the theaters but seen as propaganda by isolationists and our enemies.

1945: The digital computer named ENIAC is put into use. The machine weighs thirty tons. Its six primary programmers are all women.

1946: Cleveland Cathedral Latin plays Cleveland Holy Name on November 23, 1946, in front of 70,955.

1946: At the end of the war, five thousand television sets are being used in the United States, and by the next year, thirteen different commercial televisions would be available to the public. By 1951, 17 million had been sold.

1947: Levittown, the first planned suburb of uniformed tract homes, springs up in New York and caters to ex-servicemen who purchased their first home with GI benefits and started their families.

1948: Because of the continued growth of Jewish refugees and settlers to Israel during the war, the region becomes embroiled in what would become the Arab-Israeli War.

1949: The population by the end of the decade is 132,122,000.

1949: NASCAR starts its Grand National racing series, and the Ladies Professional Golf Association (LPGA) is born.

THE 1950s

MASSILLON AND CANTON McKINLEY DOMINATE OHIO

Tiger: a. a fierce or aggressive person or quality;
b. one (as a situation) that is formidable or impossible to control.

Bulldog: tenacious, never quits, a winner.

Kendal, Ohio, was founded in 1812 by a group of new-agers seeking a place where they could escape structured life and live an idealized existence—kind of like the communes we know from the 1960s. It didn't last long, and after a while, the folk moved a little closer to the Tuscarawas River and together with the villages of West Massillon (1831) and Massillon proper (1826) incorporated as the city of Massillon in 1853 (named after Jean Baptiste Massillon, who, as a French Catholic preacher more than one hundred years earlier, was known for his oratory and his desire for equality for all men). Kendal's relocation closer to the river was a shrewd move.

Canton, Ohio, was founded in 1805 but for many years remained a small village several miles east of Massillon. The developers of the Ohio and Erie Canals thought it a sound idea to bring the new thoroughfare through Canton, but the town leaders refused, thinking that the canal would be dangerous to their health because of the standing water. The canal was offered to their neighbor, Kendal, and the town accepted. It turned out that Canton's fears were unfounded, and the canal improved the health of Kendal because the construction drained the nearby swamps of bad water and the disease-carrying creatures living there. The decision brought an economic boom to Kendal/Massillon, while Canton continued with its bad choices by not allowing a railroad to come through the town (the residents were asked to pledge $10,000) and instead letting nearby Alliance, Ohio, enjoy the resultant prosperous growth after it accepted the offer. Massillon opened warehouses and started shipping grain to Lake Erie, and later, when coal mines were started up close by, the shipping of that commodity to steamship companies and steel mills near the big lake added additional riches to the youthful community. Successes continued: when Russell & Company opened in the early 1850s, it became the world's largest producer of steam engines. Massillon was doing quite nicely, thank you.

For Canton, these were temporary setbacks. It ultimately found a niche in manufacturing farm implements and became rich and busy when those businesses blossomed, shipping their products to countries all around the world. Later in the 1800s, Canton became a center for watch manufacturing, iron and steel. Both Massillon and Canton, as they entered the 1890s, enjoyed strong economies and stable populations, and in 1894, it was time for the two cities to meet each other on the gridiron, a term newly applied to the rectangular field where American football was now played, so named because of its horizontal lines and its resemblance to a metal grate used for years over open fires or in fireplaces to cook food. That very same cooking gridiron would attain its own special niche in future football history by its ubiquitous presence at tribal-like tailgating rituals and raucous halftime parties.

Massillon Washington Tigers

World War II veteran Coach Chuck Mather of the Massillon Washington Tigers had joined this singular football behemoth in 1948, an outsider who had not come up through the ranks of Massillon subordinate schools and teams. From Hopewell, Ohio, and just thirty-three, he had brought with him some interesting ideas and concepts that worked well—so well, in fact, that in his first two years he went 18-2, losing to Alliance in 1948 and Mansfield Senior in 1949 but coming away with enough votes to take home the state crown each time. In the next four seasons that he was coach of the Tigers, he would lose only one more game.

In an article posted online on October 15, 2017, by Joe Scalzo for www.cantonrep.com, he recorded some comments by players on Coach Mather's teams of this era. Chuck Vliet, one of many outstanding players Mather coached and someone who was the team defensive captain in 1951, said that the coach stressed technique all the time. Vliet said, "Mather treated us like gentlemen. He worked our tails off, but he never cursed. If we made a mistake, he'd ask in a calm voice, 'Why aren't you doing that this way?'"

Lee Nussbaum, a second-team All-Ohio running back in 1952 who played one season for combustible Ohio State coach Woody Hayes, said, "I played under Mather for four years and he never cussed me out, never raised his voice at me. Never raised hell. Then, when I went down to play for Woody, I thought, 'What the hell did I get myself into?'"

Scalzo wrote that Mather didn't ease up during the season either. Players couldn't smoke or drive. They were expected to be in bed by 9:00 p.m. Practices were grueling, with Mather believing that if you wanted to play in Friday's game, you had to prove it in practice. "We got so tired of beating each other up, that we couldn't wait for Friday night," Vliet said. It's what it took.

Massillon Washington's schedule during these years was a roster of some of the most historic teams in Ohio, teams who had proven track records of success, who didn't back down from anyone and would play anywhere. They attracted boys from everywhere in their hometowns to play for them, much like colleges do today, because they were the best around and played the best. And Massillon Washington was the team all of them wanted to play and be measured against. It's just the way it was and still is today.

1950

First up for the Tigers in 1950, the year we entered the conflict with North Korea, was Akron Central, a school from the Rubber City that had won multiple Akron City Series championships since beginning play in 1911. A proud school with great traditions, this was not to be its year or the best game to rekindle the glory of the past—Coach Mather's Tigers whipped Akron Central, 49–0, on a Friday night, September 15.

Next for the Tigers was Canton Lincoln, which had been co-champion of Ohio in 1945, sharing the title with Toledo Waite High School. Like Central, time had not kept pace with that past glory, and Massillon left the field that night with a 46–0 win.

Cleveland Cathedral Latin, an immensely strong school with a history almost as awe-inspiring as Washington, was kicked around and defeated by Mather's fast and strong men 62–0! Not a game anyone wants on their résumé.

The Big Red of Steubenville High School, under the second-year leadership of Coach Ray Hyman, were on the schedule to play football with Massillon Washington in the Tigers' fourth game of the year. The Big Red gridders were never easy to beat, and the boys from alongside the Ohio River fought hard but still lost, 35–12.

The Alliance Aviators were quarterbacked by All-Ohioan John Borton and were 3-1 when they trotted onto the field to play the Tigers. They had already beaten three teams convincingly, but in their most recent game they lost to the Barberton Magics, 20–0. Coached by Mel Knowlton, the Aviators were always a tough play and hoped to recover from the loss in the previous game. They didn't—Washington won, 29–7.

Mansfield Senior lost 56–6 in the next game, and the score speaks for itself. This victory avenged a 16–12 loss to Senior the previous year that knocked Massillon Washington from the undefeated ranks and left it at 9-1.

Warren Harding is a notable Buckeye team. The Raiders from over in Trumbull County had had an up-and-down legacy since starting play in

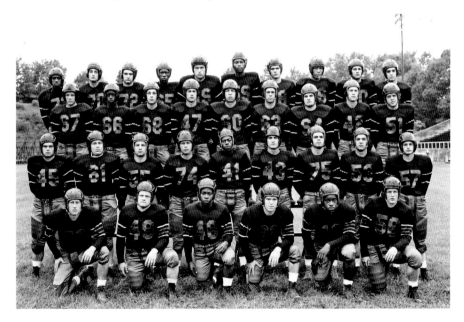

The 1950 Canton McKinley Bulldogs. *Courtesy Canton City Schools.*

1892 but had gone 8-2 the previous year and were not doing so good this year (ending the 1950 season at 6-5 and having last beaten the Tigers in 1947 by a score of 20–13). Coach Mather and his gang realized that they wouldn't just roll over and fought hard to defeat the Raiders, 23–6, the closest game of the year so far for the Tigers. It was also a portent of things to come.

The last three games were victories as well: 39–0 against Toledo Waite, 35–6 against Barberton and, in the big finale, 33–0 against the Bulldogs of Canton McKinley.

The year 1950 was an almost perfect season for the Tigers, going undefeated and winning the state and national championships of high school football in the process. These teams Washington beat were not patsies, and the impressive nature of the advantage was convincing. But that Warren Harding game—something about it was worrisome to Mather.

1950 OHIO AP STATE POLL

1. Massillon (10-0) (also National Champions)—defeated Steubenville, Canton McKinley
2. Hamilton (9-1)
3. Barberton (8-1)
4. Springfield (8-1-1)
5. Upper Arlington (10-0)
6. Portsmouth (7-2-1)
7. New Philadelphia (9-0-1)
8. Canton McKinley (7-3)—lost to Massillon, Steubenville, Toledo Waite
9. Steubenville (8-2)—lost to Massillon and Weirton (West Virginia)
10. Lakewood (10-0)

1951

Massillon

The Tigers attacked their schedule for 1951, beating their first two opponents convincingly before meeting up with Steubenville and Ohio Lineman of the Year, Calvin Jones, surviving this contest to come away with a 13–6 win. They soundly defeated Akron South in the next game, 54–13, as Tigers sophomore John Francisco (five-foot-ten, 180 pounds) scored six touchdowns on runs of 1, 22, 23, 8, 25 and 31 yards on only nine carries. He later went to Kansas, becoming one of the first African American players to play football for the Jayhawks and lettering in 1955–57. They next beat Alliance, 34–21, but not without some sweat.

Mansfield Senior, a team who had beaten Massillon Washington before but had gotten thumped in 1950, once again got their bell rung to an almost identical score from that year, losing 54–0. Clearly the Mansfield version of the Tigers (called the Tygers) needed some new blood in their pack to compete with their bigger and faster kin.

Heading into the next game with Warren Harding, the Massillon Washington players must have been confident after the shellacking they had given opponents up to that point (the Steubenville game aside).

Coach Charles Riffle of Warren Harding had joined their school system as head football coach in 1949 and took the team to a 3-7-1 record before improving them to 6-5 in 1950. His guys were having a better year and would end up 8-3, one of those wins being this game with Massillon Washington, a huge 19–13 victory that stunned the Tigers and just about everyone else who thought they would roll along once more with no trouble. A notable display

Vicious hitting at full speed without facemasks—Massillon versus Canton McKinley, November 17, 1951. *Courtesy Canton City Schools.*

of defensive football took place in this contest: Massillon's Chuck Vliet set a school record by getting thirty-two tackles, an outstanding accomplishment that still stands at the time of this writing.

The Tigers bounced back with three straight shutouts to end the season and win the state title again, but they must have been feeling the effects of that Warren Harding loss, for they just got by Barberton in the next to last game by a score of only 6–0. Then they whipped Canton McKinley, 40–0, to close out the season.

Presenting the Barberton Magics

As you can see in the 1951 AP Poll, the Barberton Magics finished 6th in the final polling, having lost only to Massillon, 6–0, in the next-to-last game that year. Aside from the touchdown, the Tigers were in the Magics' territory just one other time. Only a goal line stand by Massillon prevented Barberton from scoring and possibly winning the game. Barberton beat the Tigers in a statistical battle. Both teams left all their blood, sweat and tears on the field.

1951 BARBERTON MAGICS RECORD
Akron East, 12-6
Akron South, 14-0
Akron Garfield, 27-0
Alliance, 12-7
Elyria, 27-6
Canton Lincoln, 6-0
Akron St. Vincent, 14-7
Cuyahoga Falls, 27-7
Massillon, 0-6

Barberton High School started its virginal football program in 1904 with two games—one win and one loss. The first was at Massillon on Friday, October 14, 1904, and the team got beat by the Tigers, 15–0. The second game was at home, and they came out a winner against Akron Central (later Akron High School), 17–0.

In these early years, Barberton played several of the area teams, including many from the Akron City League and from Stark County, and birthed some tremendous athletes, a prime example being the six-foot-three, 190-pound

Frank Goettge (pronounced "getchy"), who was born in Canton but later moved to Barberton and attended Barberton High School, where, in 1913, he was the leading scorer on the Magics football team. From 1914 to 1916, he played for several semipro teams, including the Akron Burkharts, Barberton Eagles and Youngstown Patricians. He attended Ohio University for a short while and played on the freshmen Bobcats team, but with the coming of war in Europe, he enlisted in the United States Marine Corps.

Seeing combat during the Meuse-Argonne Campaign, which began on September 26, 1918, Goettge fought bravely with the Fifth Marines and was awarded a battlefield commission to lieutenant. After serving in occupation duty in Segendorf, Germany, he returned home. During the period of 1921 to 1924, he returned to his love and played football with the Quantico Marines, the team based at Quantico, Virginia. (The Marine Corps fielded a team at Quantico from 1918 to 1972 that included many NFL stars, college All-Americans, Olympic stars and Medal of Honor and Navy Cross winners, winning 335 games in that time, many against major universities.) While there, he drew huge praise from football gurus for his skills and was compared to the greatest of the time, including Jim Thorpe. The New York Giants liked what they saw and offered him a contract, but he decided that serving his country in the Corps was preferable to anything else. Barberton High School had developed a football stud as well as a dedicated defender of our country.

By 1930, he was a captain (promotion was snail-like between the wars) and a White House aide and commanded the Honor Guard for President Taft's funeral. In June 1933, Goettge served aboard the battleship *Pennsylvania* and then was assigned as commanding officer of the Marine Corps detachment at Annapolis, Maryland. In June 1941, he was assigned to the First Marine Division and was the division intelligence officer and assistant chief of staff when the division went ashore at Guadalcanal in August of the following year.

On Guadalcanal, Goettge led a famous patrol that has been described in many books and was portrayed in the movie *Guadalcanal Diary*, albeit one that ended in disaster. Using intelligence gleaned from a prisoner, a twenty-five-man patrol (three officers, twenty-one enlisted men and one navy coxswain) landed via a Higgins boat on August 12, 1942, just to the west of Guadalcanal's Matanikau River mouth thinking they were to meet some spent Japanese sailors and civilian workers wanting to surrender. Although they traveled light, just some water and ammo, one meal and a can of fish—no automatic weapons—the Japanese heard the marines and marshaled their forces, while the leathernecks prepared to defend their area on the beach. Goettge, now a lieutenant colonel, took a Captain Ringer and a First Sergeant Custer with him to recon out front. Unfortunately, they drew fire, and Goettge was shot in the head and died. The other two made it back to the beach, where, because the boat had been beached, the marines could not withdraw, although a volunteer did try to swim back for help. The marines were killed one by one throughout the night until, at dawn, only four remained alive. A second swimmer had been dispatched earlier to get reinforcements, but although he made it, as did the first man, they were too late.

The remaining marines were killed after trying to make a dash for the jungle, all except Platoon Sergeant Frank Few, who, upon striking out into the water to swim back four miles to reach friendly troops and zigzagging to avoid being killed, saw the Japanese soldiers emerge from the jungle and shoot and mutilate his comrades' bodies lying on the beach ("I saw sabers flashing in the sun," he said). Just three out of twenty-six survived. Goettge's body, among others, was never found, although later expeditions after the war tried to find them. The news of this brutal fight and the mutilation of the bodies made headlines back home, spreading throughout the Corps and hardening the marines' resolve against the Japanese, with patrols growing more aggressive and showing no quarter with few prisoners.

Frank Goettge was enshrined into the Barberton Sports Hall of Fame, the Summit County Sports Hall of Fame and the United States Marine Corps Sports Hall of Fame. He was the first football player inducted into the USMC Sports Hall of fame ahead of players like Ernie Nevers, Elroy "Crazy Legs" Hirsch and Angelo Bertelli. Seeing him play in 1921 before a crowd of sixteen thousand in Baltimore against the Army III Corps (coached by Dwight Eisenhower), the football guru Walter Camp, surely someone who knew talent, called him "one of the greatest football players in American gridiron history," saying he was "better that day than Jim Thorpe on a good day." The Goettge Memorial Field House at the giant Marine Corps base Camp Lejeune in North Carolina is named in his honor.

The 1940s had thus claimed one of Barberton's most famous athletes and premier football players. The young Barberton men who went out for the football team those crisp autumns following Colonel Goettge's supreme sacrifice surely knew his story and used his courage as a motivator. In fact, word of his death arrived in Barberton on the day before their first game in 1942. The game was dedicated to the colonel's memory. On one of the pervasive technological marvels of today, "a blog," Barberton faithful debated Goettge as the no. 3 greatest player in their history, no. 2 on the list being Billy Taylor, later an All-American at Michigan and a former NFL and CFL player, and no. 1 being Bob Toneff, a lineman for the 1947 state

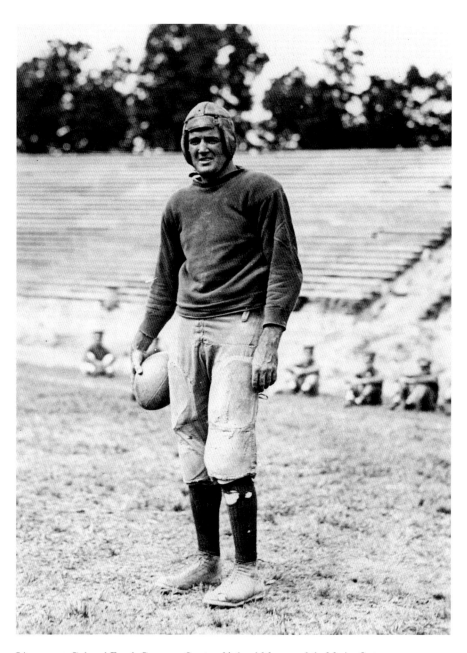

Lieutenant Colonel Frank Goettge. *Courtesy National Museum of the Marine Corps.*

championship team, Notre Dame, and Pro Bowler with the Washington Redskins and San Francisco 49ers.

Thus, the Magics that night against Massillon in 1951, losing only 6–0 against a powerful foe, might have had Goettge and the ultimate sacrifice he made at Guadalcanal in mind, playing hard up to that last play of the goal line stand.

Fremont Ross Little Giants

Fremont, Ohio, is located near Lake Erie and is the county seat of Sandusky County. Fremont High School has played football since the mid-1890s. Its main rival, the Sandusky High School Blue Streaks, is located just a few miles away adjacent to the lake; Sandusky is the county seat of Erie County. They first hit each other on November 2, 1895, with Sandusky winning, 6–0. Since that time, theirs has been one of the best and longest-lasting rivalries in the state.

The 1897 Fremont High School football team. *Courtesy Rutherford B. Hayes Presidential Center.*

The 1906 Sandusky High School football team. *Courtesy Sandusky Library.*

These two teams would go at it year after year, making their seasons if they win and enjoying bragging rights the next few months, especially when the Little Giants would win and visit Cedar Point Amusement Park in Sandusky the following summers. Much more on the Sandusky Blue Streaks in the later chapters.

In 1951, Fremont Ross would go 9-0-1 and finish 9th in the final AP Poll. It was its first undefeated season in the modern era. Its record is recounted here:

1951	Fremont Ross	39	Willoughby	7
1951	Fremont Ross	14	Lorain Senior	7
1951	Fremont Ross	26	Fostoria	0
1951	Fremont Ross	25	Findlay	21
1951	Fremont Ross	19	Sandusky	14
1951	Fremont Ross	13	Columbus East	13
1951	Fremont Ross	45	Bowling Green	27
1951	Fremont Ross	26	Elyria	7
1951	Fremont Ross	19	Toledo Scott	0
1951	Fremont Ross	32	Marion Harding	0

Coached by Mal Mackey, considered by Fremont Ross football fans the best Little Giants coach they ever had, he would take his 1950s teams to four undefeated seasons, including the longest string of consecutive wins in school history (twenty-nine from 1955 to 1957).

The 1951 Ross team, which went 9-0-1, the first undefeated mark in school history. *Courtesy Rutherford B. Hayes Presidential Center.*

The 1951 Ross backfield. *Front:* Center Charles Jones (no. 85). *Back, from left to right:* Jerome Surratt (77), Earl Asperger (87), Ron Whitcomb (71), John Lewis (73) and Charles Black (65). *Courtesy Van Ness's Time Out Sports Bar.*

1951 OHIO AP STATE POLL

1. Massillon (9-1)—defeated Steubenville, Barberton; lost to Warren Harding
2. Steubenville (9-1)—defeated Warren Harding; lost to Massillon
3. Springfield (9-1)
4. Hamilton (9-1)
5. Zanesville (9-0)
6. Barberton (8-1)—lost to Massillon
7. Warren Harding (7-3)—beat Massillon; lost to Steubenville
8. Cleveland Collinwood (9-0-1)
9. Fremont Ross (9-0-1)
10. Lima Central (8-1)

Courtesy Van Ness's Time Out Sports Bar.

1952

Massillon

Powerful, intimidating, bad-ass football players, but not perfect—that's who the 1952 Massillon eleven were. Still, you would not want to go one on one with them on some dark street. They wiped the slate clean this year but had a major scare when they played at Alliance on October 10 in front of eleven thousand insane fans. This was a game where, if you told others what had happened, they would say, "You're BSing me! That could never happen!" But it did.

Ranked no. 7 at the time, the Aviators had some veterans on the team and, to a man, did not back down. Alliance fielded hard-hitting teams every year. Just ask their opponents. They weren't scared of Massillon, especially on their home field. And after this game, it was the Aviators who came away satisfied and the Tigers who felt defeated, even though the home team lost.

Let's see what I am talking about:

- There were two consecutive kick-off returns for touchdowns, both by the Tigers.
- Both quarterbacks connected for 50 percent or better on their pass attempts, good for the era.

- Alliance made sixteen first downs to Massillon's eleven, and both ended up with the same net yardage (234).
- The final score was 27–21 Massillon.

Alliance had a quarterback by the name of Len Dawson who would go on to a stellar college and professional career and end up in the Pro Football Hall of Fame just a short distance away in Canton, Ohio. This night, even nursing an injured shoulder suffered the week before, he was phenomenal. He hit on sixteen of thirty-two passes for 220 yards and two touchdowns, punted and kicked for three extra points, scored one touchdown and kicked-off. Who does that in the twenty-first century?

1952 OHIO AP STATE POLL
1. Massillon (10-0) (also National Champions)
2. Springfield (10-0)
3. East Liverpool (9-0-1)
4. Cincinnati Purcell (9-0-1)
5. Dayton Chaminade (8-1-1)
6. Washington Court House (9-0)
7. Cleveland Benedictine (10-0)
8. Middletown (8-1-1)
9. Van Wert (10-0)
10. Youngstown Ursuline (8-1)

1953

Although Massillon caught the voters' attention again this year, winning all its games, special attention should be paid to the Portsmouth Trojans.

Portsmouth Trojans

Located down on the Ohio River, Portsmouth was for a long time an industrial town with a population peaking at about forty thousand in 1930. The Great Depression of the 1930s and other factors had an impact, and the population steadily declined during the next few decades. Portsmouth

Fremont Ross coach Mal Mackey (*left*) talks to his assistants (*from left to right*), John Ihnat, Jack Decker, Paul Raines and Robert Seele. *Courtesy Van Ness's Time Out Sports Bar.*

High School is the town's only high school and for many years had done itself proud as a basketball power, while also sending many kids off to play major-league baseball.

In 1953, the football team was blessed by the gods to go undefeated and contend for the state championship. In nine games, they scored 342 points, allowed only 42 and beat their opponents by 33 or more points per game. Their star halfback, LeRoy Carr, was selected Ohio Back of the Year, and Head Coach Bob Brownson was chosen as Ohio Coach of the Year. Two players went on to play in the pros. Trojan Leo Brown played three years for Ohio State and was captain his senior year, the first black captain at OSU. After OSU, he became an oral surgeon in the U.S. Air Force, retiring as a colonel after twenty years. Coach Ara Parseghian, then coach at Miami University, said that Miami scouts considered Portsmouth High School's football team not only the best high school team they had seen that year, but also the best team they had seen in the last five years. Pretty good endorsement!

The Little Giants of Fremont went 9-1, losing only to Massillon Washington, another great season thanks to Coach Mal Mackey and his staff.

1953 OHIO AP STATE POLL

1. Massillon (10-0) (also National Champion)—defeated Warren Harding, Fremont Ross
2. Portsmouth
3. Dayton Chaminade
4. New Philadelphia
5. Warren Harding (8-2)—lost to Massillon, Hamilton
6. Fremont Ross—lost to Massillon
7. Toledo DeVilbiss
8. Cincinnati Purcell
9. Cleveland Rhodes
10. Urbana

1954

Massillon Wins Again

The Tigers once more won the championship, with Canton McKinley regaining its moxie and contending for the top spot before losing to Massillon in the last game. The team finished third in the final AP Poll.

Canton McKinley had a rough start to the '50s, going 7-3, 2-8, 6-3-1 and then 3-6-1. In 1954, the Bulldogs turned it around and went 8-2 under second-year coach Wade Watts. They lost their second game of the

The 1954 Canton McKinley Bulldogs. *Courtesy Canton City Schools*.

Canton McKinley battles Massillon Washington on November 20, 1954. *Courtesy Canton City Schools.*

year, 7–6, to Warren Harding and then handled everyone after that until meeting Massillon in the last game, which they lost, 26–6. They lost to their rival, yes, but set the tone with this turnaround for an astounding two years to come.

While we admire dynasties, many times the rest of the Top 10s have the best stories.

Cleveland Cathedral Latin Lions

Cathedral Latin School was founded in 1916 in Cleveland as an all-male Catholic preparatory school. In 1946, its football team played in the annual Charity Game against Holy Name in front of 70,955 fans in Cleveland Municipal Stadium. This game, between the East and West Senate division champions, aided Plain Dealer Charities, an organization from the local newspaper giant. The city had created a league of four Catholic and thirteen public schools, divided into the East and West Senate, that fell within its city limits; it was a struggle each year to earn the division titles and play in the Charity Game.

The 1954 team beat other teams into the ground, week after week—by a lot of points, in the forties many times, including a 58, a 61 and a 74 end-of-game total. The defense also shut out six straight opponents. They had lost just one game in two seasons by a total of 1 point and beat Holy Name once more in the '54 Charity Game.

Ranked 5th in the final AP Poll, they were the first undefeated team in the rankings. So, why not no. 1?

Jackson High School Ironmen

Jackson County and the schools therein, located in the southeastern part of Ohio, have been playing football for quite some time: Jackson since 1898, Wellston since 1908 and Oak Hill since 1919. They are three of the surviving high schools in the county once blessed with many more.

In 1952, Jackson hired Coach Gene Slaughter away from South Point, Ohio. His first year he went 7-5-0, and then he put some high octane into the system and sprinted to 36-3-1 before going on to a 76-11-3 total record. The Jackson Ironmen in 1954 went undefeated, one of five undefeated teams in that year's Top 10, yet not one of them were in the Top Four.

This year, 1954, Jackson and Wellston lined up and hit each other as undefeated teams, each ranked among the Top 10. The conference championship, was, of course, also on the line. Woody Hayes from Ohio State watched on as Jackson won, 21–6, and for the second year in a row beat its rival, the Wellston Golden Rockets.

Jackson and Wellston had met each Thanksgiving since the Southeastern Ohio Athletic League was formed, with both Jackson and Wellston as members, in 1925. This day was their last Thanksgiving game.

Wellston, who had hired a new head coach, Ben Wilson, led the 1951 team to the school's only 10-0-0 season, although the team won just two of their games by one point. In '53 and '54, they lost only to Jackson. Wilson's career path took him later in life to lead the 1970 Wichita State team; tragically, half the team, as well as Wilson's wife, perished in a plane crash (one of two carrying the team) while en route to play Utah State University. Then, six weeks later, a plane carrying the Marshall University football team also crashed. Wichita State did not play the scheduled game at Utah State but did complete the season under the leadership of Assistant Coach Bob Seaman, the former head coach at Sandusky High School and Massillon Washington.

On Thursday, October 28, 2016, the 2,177[th] and final Southeastern Ohio Athletic League football game was played, between the Logan Chieftains and the Warren Warriors. The state's oldest, continually operating non-city league had been formed on March 7, 1925, at the Rogan Hotel in Wellston, Ohio. The original members were Athens, Gallipolis, Ironton, Jackson, Logan, Nelsonville, Oak Hill, Portsmouth and Wellston.

1954 OHIO AP STATE POLL

1. Massillon (9-1)—defeated Canton McKinley, Mansfield; lost to Alliance
2. Alliance (9-1)—defeated Massillon; lost to Canton McKinley
3. Canton McKinley (8-2)—defeated Springfield, Alliance; lost to Massillon
4. Mansfield (9-1)
5. Cleveland Cathedral Latin (10-0)
6. Youngstown Rayen (9-0)
7. Lancaster (9-0)
8. Jackson (9-0)
9. Springfield (8-2)—lost to Canton McKinley
10. Cincinnati Elder (9-0)

1955

Massillon Interruptus!: Canton McKinley

It was 1955 and Massillon Washington High School had just won seven straight state championships. Could it go on forever? Many believed so, not the least of which were the Tigers themselves. But the Bulldog players over at their chief rival, McKinley High School, a few miles away in Canton, Ohio, thought differently.

Massillon, Ohio, supported just one public high school during its long history, while Canton, Ohio, supported four (McKinley, Lehman, Lincoln and Timken) up to the 1975 football season. A change was not going to begin until the Bulldogs beat the Tigers and kept on beating them to ensure that each fan's emotions got heated to the boiling point. In 1955, the Bulldogs were loaded with talent and ready to make it happen.

Canton McKinley versus Akron South. *Courtesy www.cantonrep.com.*

The Canton McKinley team decimated all who lined up in front of them, forcing four shutouts and whipping a perennial southeast Ohio power in Steubenville. At the end of the year, for the last game, with so many of the seniors who had worked so hard and endured beatings from that team down the road (just eight miles away), they were more than ready to take Massillon on.

On a cold, wet and icy Fawcett Stadium field in Canton, the Bulldogs and the Tigers fought heroically through mud, wind and snow to a point when the twenty-two thousand fans and the players themselves could not tell the teams apart, being so encrusted with the slop. It was so bad that only ball handling mistakes could probably dictate who the winner might be, and it turned out to be just so. Two punt snaps by Massillon were mishandled and led to the Bulldogs putting enough points on the board to come away with a 13–7 victory. One snap was recovered in the end zone for a score, while the second needed three tries by Napoleon "Nap" Barbosa to get in for the touchdown. The extra point to put McKinley ahead, 7–0, was good.

Don Duke of Massillon tied it up at 7–7, and the half ended. In the last quarter, Bill White of the Bulldogs jumped on another high Massillon snap in the end zone for a touchdown. The extra point was missed, and that was it. Oddly, the extremely potent Bulldog offense was checked the

The Bulldogs whip Massillon in 1955. *Courtesy Canton City Schools.*

entire game by Massillon, and the Tigers won the statistical battle but lost the game. It didn't matter to the Canton McKinley Bulldogs, though, as they left the field winners.

In recognition of his football talent, McKinley's Napoleon Barbosa, the hero of the Massillon game, was inducted into the McKinley Football Hall of Fame and the Canton Negro Old Timers Hall of Fame in the 1980s.

This defeat at Canton, combined with a 12–12 tie with Mansfield Senior (which Massillon tied with just two seconds left in the game), doomed the Massillon Tigers from winning yet another state championship and catapulted the Canton McKinley Bulldogs to the 1955 state crown.

The 1955 Canton McKinley/Massillon game is still talked about today and will continue to be so until Ohio High School football is no more.

1955 CANTON MCKINLEY SCHEDULE

Cleveland Lincoln	W 71–0
at Warren Harding	W 46–0
Toledo Scott	W 52–0
Canton Lincoln	W 74–7
Akron East	W 25–7
Steubenville	W 34–6

at Alliance	W 30–6
at Toledo Waite	W 29–7
Akron South	W 22–0
Massillon Washington	W 13–7

Upper Sandusky High School Rams

Upper Sandusky High School in Wyandot County, an almost equal distance between Toledo and Columbus, can probably call 1955 one of its greatest in football, if not the greatest. Coached by Leo Strang, the Rams went 9-0 and finished 9th in the final AP Poll. They outscored their opponents, 329–89, and won the Northern Ohio League title. They won their next league title in 2003, and three grandchildren of players from the 1955 team played on the 2003 team.

Coach Strang, a three-year navy veteran of World War II, was a graduate of Ashland High School and Ashland College in Ohio. He went 35-10 in five years coaching the Rams before going on to coach East Cleveland Shaw in 1956. He went 16-3 before going to Massillon Washington High School to coach the mighty Tigers. There he would win state championships and become famous, becoming the first coach to let his team wear colored shoes and decals on the helmets. They won, of course, a lot. But it was that 9-0 Upper Sandusky squad that launched him upward. That little town in Wyandot County will always remember him.

Fremont Ross Little Giants

Coming in 4th in the final AP Poll was Fremont Ross. Undefeated, along with several other teams, it was a good year for high school football in Ohio. Whether Fremont and East Liverpool should have been above Massillon in the rankings is open to debate, but the Little Giants were *big* this year in a highly competitive run to the final poll.

1955 FREMONT ROSS SCHEDULE

1955	Fremont Ross	20	Lima Senior		6
1955	Fremont Ross	7	Hammond, IN, Bishop Noll		0
1955	Fremont Ross	30	Fostoria		0
1955	Fremont Ross	27	Findlay		6

1955	Fremont Ross	20	Sandusky	6
1955	Fremont Ross	19	Elyria	6
1955	Fremont Ross	28	Lorain Senior	0
1955	Fremont Ross	30	Marion Harding	12
1955	Fremont Ross	12	Toledo Scott	0
1955	Fremont Ross	28	Portsmouth	20

1956

Canton McKinley Does It Again!

After Canton McKinley's 1955 state championship season culminating in a home win against Massillon Washington, the two teams were primed for another go at each other. Both teams were talented with experienced players heading into 1956. But the story of their respective seasons followed different tracks and would lead to a season-ending clash of titans.

McKinley rolled over every team it played, with scores like 80–6, 60–12 and 66–13. Massillon had a tougher time of it, winning games, but with closer scores. The one setback was at Mansfield Senior, where it lost, 14–6, on October 9. In another strange game that can only be played in high school, the Mansfield Tygers ran seventy-five plays to Massillon's thirty-four. Massillon outgained Mansfield 312 yards to 292 yards. Massillon had a 27-yard touchdown pass called back due to a penalty, and Mansfield's running backs took advantage of poor tackling by the Tigers to get extra yards after the initial hits. It was just one of those nights when an extra effort, a quicker step or a stretch of another inch in several instances would have given Massillon a win. But it just wasn't to be.

So, heading into the all-important last game on its home field against the Bulldogs, Massillon had a lot on the line. Get a convincing win against the reigning state champs and the team might win enough poll votes to sneak into 1st place and snag another state title.

On November 17, 1956, the Canton McKinley Bulldogs trotted out onto Tiger Stadium's field under a roar of twenty-three thousand fans from both communities. Up to this point, many had touted this Bulldog team as one of the best-ever produced in Canton and maybe Ohio. The way they had whipped all who lined up against them was sure proof. But this was Massillon, and although the Tigers had stumbled, you could

The 1956 Canton McKinley football team. *Courtesy Canton City Schools.*

Wayne Fontes of Canton McKinley carries the ball against Massillon. *Courtesy Canton City Schools.*

not count any Massillon team out until the gun was fired at the end of the game.

Canton's quarterback, Ike Grimsley, had one of his best games, and receiver Bobby Williams, an exceptional athlete who had scored ten touchdowns during the season, intercepted two Massillon passes and recovered a fumble. Bulldog halfback Phil Martin scored on runs of 5, 55 and 77 yards. Wayne Fontes, a future Michigan State star and college/pro coach, carried sixteen times for 95 yards for McKinley. Grimsley kept it fourteen times and gained 81 yards. Massillon could not get untracked and lost, 34–7.

The Bulldogs were tough in 1955 and 1956. They were extremely fast, and in an article about the 1956 team by Steve Doerschuk of www.cantonrep. com, posted on June 25, 2017, halfback Phil Martin said that Coach Wade Watts ignored weightlifting, which helped keep their injuries to a minimum. Wayne Fontes said, "He did a good job organizing what he wanted done." He allowed QB Ike Grimsley to call his own plays. Watts even created a triple-option offense before it became popular. The coach told his team, "If you hit them harder than they hit you, you won't get hurt."

Canton McKinley beats Massillon for the second straight year on November 17, 1956. Ike Grimsley launches a pass. *Courtesy Canton City Schools.*

They practiced on a field everyone called "hard as a rock," and some did not wear face masks. Those who did wear a single bar remember them repeatedly breaking and felt lucky that they did not injure their faces. Toughness, teamwork, shared misery—it's what it took.

1956 CANTON MCKINLEY SCHEDULE

Cleveland Lincoln	W 80–6
Warren Harding	W 60–12
at Barberton	W 61–0
Canton Lincoln	W 33–14
Toledo Waite	W 34–0
at Steubenville	W 66–13
Alliance	W 21–7
Toledo Scott	W 46–0
Akron South	W 55–7
at Massillon Washington	W 34–7

1956 OHIO AP STATE POLL

1. Canton McKinley (10-0)—defeated Massillon
2. Fremont Ross (10-0)
3. Mansfield (9-0)—defeated Massillon
4. Cleveland St. Ignatius (9-1)
5. Youngstown Ursuline (10-0)
6. Cleveland Benedictine (6-2)—lost to Massillon
7. Lorain (7-1-1)
8. Massillon (8-2)—defeated Cleveland Benedictine; lost to Canton McKinley, Mansfield
9. Troy (9-0)
10. East Liverpool (8-2)

Achieving 10-0 records in 1955 and 1956, McKinley's football team beat Massillon twice in a row for the first time since 1933 (unfortunately, after these two wins, the Bulldogs lost the next seven in the series—at this point, the series stood 29 wins, 27 losses and 5 ties in Washington's favor); beat Stark County rivals Canton Lincoln, Alliance and Massillon by a combined score of 88–28; scored a school-record 490 points in 1956; and won the state title two years in a row—a first.

McKinley's coach, Wade Watts, was UPI's Coach of the Year in 1955 and 1956. After the 1957 season, Coach Watts took a job at a California high school.

The following information from an article posted on June 25, 2017, by Steve Doerschuck on www.cantonrep.com on Stark County's players vividly shows how Massillon and Canton, as well as other Stark County teams, were just plain good these two years:

> *In 1955, the All-Ohio first team included McKinley's Williams and Alliance tackle Larry Long on offense and McKinley linebacker Ronnie Perdue, McKinley defensive back Nap Barbosa, Massillon end Jim Houston and Lehman end Dick Gelesky on defense. Barbosa also was McKinley's quarterback.*
>
> *The '55 second team included McKinley end Herman Jackson on offense and Massillon end Dave Canary, Jackson tackle Larry Claxon and Massillon linebacker Don Duke on defense.*
>
> *The 11-man, first-team, All-Ohio offense for 1956 included quarterback Ike Grimsley, running back Wayne Fontes and end Bobby Williams of McKinley as well as Alliance center Curt Binkley. Massillon's quarterback, Mike Hershberger, made first-team, All-Ohio on defense.*
>
> *The 11-man, second-team, All-Ohio offense included Lincoln end Larry Ellison, Massillon tackle Jim Mercer and Timken guard Don Meister. McKinley's Phil Martin was on the second team defense as a safety.*

Massillon Washington and Canton McKinley ruled Ohio's football landscape for nine straight years. The Massillon Washington Tigers won every year from 1948 to 1954. The Bulldogs won in 1955 and '56. The players selected in the previous article were really an All-Ohio team, as there were no classes or divisions yet. But both would have to wait for a repeat, as three other teams sought claim to the state title and they all would have unique stories to tell.

1957

The Men of Cleveland Benedictine

Benedictine High School in Cleveland is a male-only, Catholic college preparatory institution. Based on the scholarly traditions of the Benedictine

Order, founded in AD 480 and the oldest religious order in the Catholic Church, it opened in 1927 and started fielding football teams in 1930. Benedictine monks still teach at the school.

In 1955, a new coach, Augie Bossu, stepped in to lead them. Coach Bossu had been the head coach of Cleveland Cathedral Latin from 1947 to 1952 before moving to Benedictine. He gave up coaching at Latin, itself a great program as we all know (having had previous undefeated seasons and championships), to go coach there as an assistant, a program he thought he could benefit from working with. It was an interesting move and one for which Bengal fans will be forever grateful. From 1952 to 1966, only Benedictine (twelve appearances) and Cathedral Latin (three) represented the East Senate in the annual Charity Game between the East and West Senate divisions in the city league. Benedictine would average 28,515 fans for those games.

Augie Bossu, a 160-pound guard, had played for Coach Elmer Layden's Notre Dame 1938 team, which won the national championship (awarded by the Dickinson System, not the wire services). He served in the army during World War II, becoming a major in the Signal Corps. He met his future wife, Florence, around this time and would have two sons and six daughters with the love of his life. After the war, he got a master's in physical education at Stanford University. Not a bad résumé to start life off with, is it?

At his previous jobs, and especially at Benedictine, Augie began to establish himself as a player's coach. That meant he was downwardly focused on them and not on putting notches on his résumé to enhance his career path. He knew football well and treated each of his players with personal respect. He was not an emotionally vocal coach, but he did let it be known when the players let him down, so they worked terribly hard not to. It was this style that endeared him to each guy on any of his teams, and not just in football—Coach Bossu also led the varsity baseball team for four decades, reaching the state final several times.

His kids had bought into this system, and it held them in good stead throughout the rough seasons ahead of them. In 1955, they had gone undefeated, going 9-0, but did not end up in the state's Top 10. The following year, they went 7-2 and ended 1956 ranked 6th in the state, with St. Ignatius coming in ahead of them at no. 4 even though the Bengals had whipped them, 47–6, in the Charity Game for the city championship. Getting ready for 1957 then, they had enough experience to make a solid run for the top spot, and Augie and his assistants prepared for it.

Augie at Notre Dame ('39). *Courtesy Notre Dame University.*

On September 13, 1957, the Bengals opened against Lakewood St. Edward, and it was an easy test for the Bengals, running away quickly and ending up with a 51–0 victory. A tougher opponent was second on the schedule, but Benedictine escaped with a close win over Cleveland East Tech in a game played on September 20—they were an East Senate team and an important victory for the Bengals, as they maintained the ball and held fast for a 19–12 final score.

Another Catholic college preparatory school from the northern part of Ohio, Ursuline High School from over in Youngstown, had been penciled in for September 27. The final score of 38–14 in favor of the Bengals was a significant one, a 24-point victory over a team with much pride and with an impressive football legacy. It was to come back to help the Bengals in a few weeks. Before that, though, a tune-up was in order.

East Senate opponent Cleveland Glenville was next, and Benedictine thrashed the Tarblooders, 47–7. It was a good win and, aside from being a Senate win, served to sharpen some of the ideas the coaching staff was preparing for the next game, against the Washington Tigers from Massillon, Ohio.

The Benedictine student newspaper, *The Bennet*, had dubbed running backs Gary Hansley as "Mr. Inside" and George Sefcik as "Mr. Outside" this season, and over at Tiger Stadium in Massillon before 14,488 attendees on a chilly October 11, these two guys showed why their fans and fellow students had placed these monikers on them.

The Tigers just did not have an answer for the Bengals on either side of the ball. On this night, when just about everything was set up for a win, Benedictine gained 262 total yards—Sefcik and Hansley accounted for 233 of those yards. Sefcik, fast with moves, was also a deadly passer and long-distance punter. He carried the ball twenty times and gained 82 yards, hit on three of four passes for 32 yards, caught one pass himself for 14 yards and averaged 40 yards on three runs. Hansley, said to look and run like an army tank, carried the ball twenty-two times and gained 105 yards; he also caught the three passes thrown by Sefcik, who was hoisted onto the shoulders of his teammates following the game.

The Bengals defense gave up 187 yards on the ground, most of those gained by Ivory Benjamin, a great Massillon back who scored the Tigers' only TD on a 50-yard burst. For the game, he carried twenty-two times for 161 yards. Bengals linemen Skufca, Zmarzly and Sczurek were instrumental in holding Benjamin and the other Tigers to just the one score.

This 13–7 win gave Augie's team a lot of statewide press and alerted those who did not realize it that the Bengals were a team to be reckoned with in 1957. Ignited by this great victory, the Bengals rolled through the remainder of the schedule. Waiting to play them for the City Championship on November 28 was, you guessed it, Cleveland St. Ignatius. The Wildcats of Cleveland St. Ignatius had lost one game so far in 1957, their opener against Cleveland Cathedral Latin, 9–0, on a September Friday evening, which just happened to be the thirteenth no less! Since that game, Coach John Wirtz had whipped his guys into an offensive and defensive machine of remarkable ability.

The St. Ignatius Wildcats offense contained a genuine star in Fred Oblak, a halfback who had scored 144 points on twenty-four touchdowns, a school record at that time. He had scored five TDs in one game twice and had gained 1,137 yards, usually being pulled when the game was beyond reach of the opponent. St. Ignatius over the past ten years had compiled a 69-18-

5 record, while the Benedictine boys had achieved a mark of 77-10-3. The Bengals had also gone 57-2-2 in the East Senate, while the Wildcats had been putting up a 59-9-3 record in the West.

About thirty-two thousand fans were in Municipal Stadium that cloudy day to see Benedictine fumble twice in the first quarter. After the second miscue, they kicked a 30-yard field goal to take a 3–0 lead. The defenses kept both teams otherwise scoreless up to the halftime gun. St. Ignatius had performed brilliantly, using a nine-man line to hold the Bengals' running game to just 21 yards and no first downs! Mr. Inside and Mr. Outside were going nowhere to that point.

It was a different story in the second half. Gary Hansley of the Bengals scored their first touchdown on a 14-yard burst, and Sefcik kicked the extra point for the 7–3 lead. The Wildcats then had to punt after failing to get a first down, and it was blocked by Frank Marek, with the Bengals' Stan Szcurek recovering the bouncing ball on the 10. On their third play after the block, Hansley again crossed the goal line for his second TD! It was 14–3 after Sefcik made his second kick.

The Wildcats' bad luck went on as they fumbled, and the ball was picked up and taken in for a 55-yard score by the Bengals' Frank Marek. But the referees called it dead at the St. Ignatius 47, and the Bengals had to run it in the hard way, with Sefcik getting the touchdown after a strong drive. He missed his first kick of the day, however, and it was now 20–3. The Wildcats got a touchback in the fourth quarter when Hansley was crossing the goal line for a TD and fumbled into the end zone, where it was recovered by Tom Ottman of St. Ignatius.

With fifteen seconds left in the game, Hansley scored his third touchdown of the day from four yards out, a drive ignited by an interception by Larry Hradisky. Sefcik made the extra point, and the game ended with a 27–6 victory for Augie and his Bengal team.

The Wildcat offense was stymied by the Bengals' defense in the second half, never getting beyond the 50 in the third quarter and only as far as the 45 in the fourth. All four touchdowns made by the Bengals came after Wildcat turnovers. Gary Hansley, who scored three TDs, was voted the game's MVP. Considered by more than a few the best backfield in school history, Sefcik and Hansley finished their careers as the top two scorers in school history. Sefcik's 233 points still ranks fourth on the all-time list. Hansley's 216 points are good enough for sixth place.

The 1957 Benedictine High School football season demonstrated that great coaching combined with superior talent can make for a champion.

Sometimes if you only have one or the other, you can't do it; sometimes egos and arrogance get in the way. In this case, Augie's team of 1957 put all that stuff aside and focused on the common goal of winning—everything else was secondary. It is arguably the best example of this combination (great coaching and talent) ever seen.

Augie Bossu died on January 1, 2008, at the age of ninety-one. This guy was an unbelievable person, coach, mentor and friend to all. Mike Easler, a former Bengals baseball player of great skill who had a .293 batting average in fourteen Major League seasons, said, "Bossu was the best instructor I had on any level. He coached you like you were a professional, but treated you like you were his son."

Tony Russ, who was Benedictine's AD and had played and coached with Augie, said, "We weren't afraid of him. We were afraid of disappointing him." "He wasn't a yeller," he added. "He hired assistants to do that. He was quiet and mild mannered. In the time I coached with him, I probably saw him question officials three times. He didn't berate you and point fingers at you. He told you what he wanted and if you didn't do it, he let you know that you disappointed him."

It was mentioned earlier that Augie also coached baseball. His overall record of 681-300 over forty years is excellent, and while winning those games, they won thirteen East Senate championships, twenty-three sectional titles and eleven district crowns and made five trips to the state tournament Final Four.

The great Augie Bossu is a member of the Monongahela (Pennsylvania) High School Sports Hall of Fame, the Benedictine Athletic Hall of Fame, the Ohio High School Football Coaches Hall of Fame and the Baseball Coaches Hall of Fame. He was inducted into the National High School Sports Hall of Fame in Kansas City, Missouri, in the same class as Len Dawson and Jim Taylor.

Augie was living in Maple Heights, Ohio, when he died and had remained on the Benedictine staff as the school's freshman football coach through the 2005 season, after having stepped down as varsity coach on March 1, 1994, but he continued to do some ad hoc scouting for the varsity guys. He gave up his position as junior varsity baseball coach after the 2001 season. Due to some health problems, he took a break from his activities in the summer of 2006 and did not return. He never quit attending the varsity football games, however, continuing to do so through the 2007 season.

Augie Bossu, one of this state's greatest coaches (310-130-20 in football, 681-300 in baseball). Please remember him.

1957 OHIO AP STATE POLL
1. Cleveland Benedictine (9-0)—defeated Massillon
2. Massillon (8-1)—defeated Warren Harding; lost to Cleveland Benedictine
3. Toledo DeVilbiss
4. Warren Harding (9-1)—lost to Massillon
5. Youngstown South (9-0)
6. Troy (9-0)
7. Fremont Ross (9-0-1)
8. East Cleveland Shaw (9-1)
9. Cincinnati Purcell (8-1-1)
10. Toledo Central

1958

Marion, Ohio: A Little History

Marion, Ohio, is the county seat of Marion County and was the home of Warren G. Harding, the twenty-ninth president of the United States, who campaigned from the front porch of his home, a place where he hosted famous entertainers from both coasts and promised a "return to normalcy" after the tumultuous years of World War I. A few counties north of Columbus, Marion was born, so to speak, during the War of 1812, when surveyor Jacob Foos, part of General William Henry Harrison's army, late at night and very thirsty with no water around, started digging a well on a hill where he and others were encamped and found it four feet down. Forever known as Jacob's Well, the town itself was established just north of the site in 1822 by Eber Baker, who named it in honor of General Francis Marion, the renowned "Swamp Fox" of Revolutionary War lore. General Marion, who hailed from South Carolina by the way, is the second-most honored personality from that conflict behind George Washington for places named after him. The village was incorporated over the winter of 1829–30, and the first mayor, Nathan Peters, was elected, with founder Eber Baker elected as a trustee. Marion was on its way.

Alliance, Ohio: A Little History

Alliance, Ohio, lies astride both Stark and Mahoning Counties in northwest Ohio, an area all readers should realize is probably the number one area in any state for birthing great high school football teams. Nicknamed the "Carnation City" and home to small college titan Mount Union College, Alliance was created in 1854 when three local communities came together with Mount Union joining the triumvirate in 1888, becoming a city, Alliance, the following year.

History shows us that the first Alliance football games were played in 1896. In 1917, the Aviators played East Palestine and, in a farcical outcome, whipped their opponent, 141–0, one of those games that you just cannot comprehend, no matter how long you've been watching this game.

The Alliance team had some pretty good years over the first half of the century, beating Massillon in 1932, 30–6, en route to an 11-0-1 record. (The previous meeting in 1928, in which Alliance beat Massillon, 13–0, ended in a huge brawl—got to love those Stark County boys!) That football team was coached by George Wilcoxon, later a PhD, who had previously gained fame in 1928 coaching the Aviators basketball team when they beat Massillon, 3–2, getting the game into *Ripley's Believe It or Not!* and leading to rule changes placing a time restriction on the offensive possession in the backcourt. 3–2…amazing!

In the late 1940s, after having had a terrible season of 1-8-1, the Aviators brought in a new coach, Mel Knowlton, a man who had worked for Paul Brown at Massillon (many Brown assistants became head coaches), had been a former head coach at Steubenville and was a three-year veteran of the armed forces. Knowlton knew his stuff and quickly earned a reputation as a coach who got every little bit out of each player, much more than he ever expected. Winning became commonplace once again, and Coach Knowlton gained further notoriety for developing quarterbacks such as All-Ohioans Len Dawson (later of Purdue and Kansas City Chiefs fame), John Bolton, Walt Zingg and Bob Wallace. He would coach the Alliance High School team from 1946 to 1969 and ended up with a 150-86-7 record. But it is 1958 we're talking about here, and that summer he and the Aviators were coming off a 6-2-1 record and wondering about his team's prospects for the coming year.

Let's Get Started!

The story of the 1958 Ohio race to a high school football championship is one of opportunity. Canton McKinley was not a factor this year, and there were only three undefeated teams in the final AP Top 10 and four in the UPI Top 10—and they were not all the same teams. It was a race of who was left standing and, probably, how many voters from either wire service was from what part of the state. There were new teams to be heard from, and the central part of the state was beginning to challenge northeastern Ohio. It was wide open this year, and the week-to-week story of the Alliance Aviators and the Marion Harding Presidents is just as exciting as any race in Ohio's history.

Harding's first game of the 1958 season was against Cleveland Glenville, which it easily won, 32–0. New this year was the 2-point extra point rule, which Harding used to its advantage.

Co-captain Bob Middleton was all over the field in this game and set the tone for the aggressive and relentless play that he and the rest of the defense was to show all season. Combined with co-captain Rocky Evans, the Prexies, with several others bringing outstanding efforts to bear, made a statement this night that was going to reverberate around Ohio.

The Akron Central Wildcats were the first foe for the Alliance Aviators, and Coach Knowlton went into the contest curious about his defense, all of whom were new and untested. But that did not deter 6,800 fans from entering Mount Union's Hartshorn Stadium for their first game of the season. They saw a sluggish, unexciting game that Alliance won, 22–0. The defense held up.

The bus in which the Harding team traveled to Fostoria must have continued onto the Fostoria football field because it didn't seem to stop all night, with the Presidents scoring on their first four possessions and not giving up a single point. Harding ultimately won, 48–12, and the bus that was on the field that September 19 evening accumulated 427 very offensive yards against just 168 for the Redmen while running up nineteen first downs to just eight for the home team.

Bobby Brown made the play of the game in the next Alliance game when they went to Cuyahoga Falls and won 28–12 in a rough, tough football contest indicative of northeastern Ohio. Soon to come were the Massillon Tigers.

In their first Buckeye Conference game of the year against Lorain High School, Harding led 24–8 at the half and went on to a 30–20 win, the team enduring a let-up in themselves and an energized Lorain defense.

Left: Marion Harding letter sweater. *Courtesy Marion Harding High School.*

Below: *Courtesy Alliance Historical Society, Alliance, Ohio. Reprinted from* Alliance High School's Greatest Football Teams 1980 Reunion Booklet.

1958 State Champions (9-0-1)

ALLIANCE AVIATORS
1958
STATE CHAMPIONS

Right: Aviator defense rules! *Courtesy Canton Repository*.

Below: Lee Woolf finds a hole! *Courtesy Canton Repository*.

The Tigers from Washington High School in Massillon were an undefeated high school football team when they pulled into the parking lot of Hartshorn Stadium in Alliance and began to unload their equipment.

Prior to this game, Massillon Washington had beaten Akron South, 28–0, and Canton Lincoln, 20–0. The Tigers were a big, strong team, and the Alliance paper that week said the game would be one of speed versus power, with Massillon this year not demonstrating the speed they usually bring to the table. The Aviators would have to be the faster team tonight if they wanted to win.

Coach Knowlton explains what he wants. *Courtesy Canton Repository.*

Massillon won the toss and received the kickoff, but by the end of the first quarter, it was Alliance ahead, 8–0. The half ended that way as well. The Tigers kicked off to the Aviators to start the second half, but the offense sputtered, and they punted rather quickly. The Tigers from Massillon Washington High School then went seventeen plays to score their first TD of the evening.

Highlighted by strong running by the backfield, the Tigers' Dave Dean finally crossed the Aviators' goal from just a few inches out. Jim Snively rammed across tackle for the conversion and the tie. The Massillon supporters erupted with cheers, pats on the back and fists pumping in the air, thinking now that their team was now going to roll up the Aviators just as they had done so many other teams in the past. But it was not to be, and the rest of the game was one of fumbles and interceptions. The game ended in an 8–8 tie. Neither team was satisfied with the night's effort.

It was Homecoming Week for the Marion Harding players and students, and their opponent for this game was Dayton Roosevelt, a non-conference matchup stuck in between Buckeye Conference games. It was not a great showing for the Prexies in the first half and ended at 12–0 for Harding.

Rocky Evans scored a TD in the third quarter after an 81-yard drive, but it was the fourth quarter when the gloves came off and the wreckage began in earnest. Co-captain Evans intercepted a pass at the 34 thrown by Lowell

Caylor of Roosevelt and took it all the way, shaking off tacklers as he rumbled down the field. From then on, it was a route and the final score was 40–0.

The Alliance Aviators were preparing to play a team looking to break into the Top 10 when they scouted Barberton High School and devised plays the week before to stop the Magics tandem of quarterback Bob Mobley and fullback Bob Burroughs. Some worked, some didn't. The Magics rolled up 145 yards on the ground in the first half with eleven first downs, but Alliance outgained them, getting two hundred yards but only achieving six first downs. The score was 6–6 at the half, and the Aviators had had one TD called back because of a clip and then lost the ball on the 10-yard line when they fumbled! Alliance rebounded in the second half and pounded the Magics.

The game ended 28–14, and the Alliance High School football team was 3-0-1. Marion Harding was 4-0 and ready to slug it out with the 5th-ranked Elyria High School Pioneers. Going into this week, the Alliance Aviators were fourth in the Associated Press Poll and sixth in the UPI Poll. Cleveland Benedictine versus Massillon Washington was the other big game that week.

The previous season, 1957, the Pioneers had tied Marion Harding, 20–20, that game and the loss to Fremont being the only negatives in an otherwise pretty good season for the Presidents. Harding had them whipped going into the final quarter but did not take their effort to the last minute, letting Elyria catch up. Revenge was definitely on the Prexies' minds. This was the proverbial "big game."

It was hard fought all the way through. Forearms were delivered with extra mustard, and the piles were where questionable actions went unseen and were violent. This was hard-hitting, and both teams gave no quarter. At the end, however, Harding won, 22–16.

The Harding locker room was jammed after the win, and Coach Larson refused to point out any individual player, citing the entire team for a great effort. But the defense stood out, especially in the first half, when they held the 5th-ranked Pioneers to only 25 yards rushing and no first downs. Harding outgained the Pioneers in total yardage 255-180 and led in first downs sixteen to eight. Also very significant was that the Prexies recovered four out of five Pioneer fumbles. Coach Larson hinted to reporters that a newspaper writer from a northern paper might have motivated his team to greatness when it implied that Harding had played a softer schedule than the Pioneers.

Alliance was set to entertain the Irish from Youngstown Ursuline in its next game and was possibly going to come up against a new offensive look from the Youngstown team. The Irish were coming into the Alliance game having lost to the Youngstown East Golden Bears, 14–8, and were looking for improvement. They didn't find it. The Aviators whipped the Irish, 22–0.

The Findlay Trojans (3-2), under the leadership of Coach Neil Schimdt, arrived in Marion to take on the Prexies. The Trojans were losers to Lorain the previous week, 32–13, while Harding climbed into the no. 5 spot in the polls. Might Findlay think it could steal one while the Prexies napped on their laurels? A big fat *no*, according to Coach Larson, who said, "Make no mistake about it, we're going out for a win and we mean to get it. We're not going to sacrifice what we've already won by falling down now."

The Buckeye Conference looked like this at this time:

	W	L	Pt.	Op.
Harding	2	0	52	36
Lorain	2	1	67	55
Findlay	1	1	27	54
Elyria	1	1	42	22
Sandusky	1	2	58	40
Fremont	0	2	12	60

By the end of the game, the Trojans must have thought they had walked into a boxed canyon and got attacked by a war party. The Prexies gained 284 yards rushing and 138 passing for 421 total yards to Findlay's meager 147. The Marion defensive line of Bob Middleton, Mike Chamberlain, Jim Hathaway and Gary Massie was harassing the Findlay backfield and manhandling its line. The hitting was fierce, the Findlay runners' being tossed for losses of 18 yards to give them a net of just 99 on the ground—that's a long night! Harding whipped them, 38–0, and sent them home.

Harding showed off new shoes for this game: bright red low-cuts. Findlay's band made the trip but played only blues on the way home.

The Cleveland Glenville Tarblooders were the Aviators' next opponent, and Alliance could be excused if it might have been looking past them to Canton McKinley the following week. Glenville had just sustained huge losses to Cleveland Cathedral Latin and Cleveland Benedictine and was seeking a good showing against the Aviators to regain its confidence and swagger. In the first quarter, the team looked like they might do just that, the Aviators needing the last four plays of the first quarter to get their initial first down. The Alliance home crowd was impatient, and as the second quarter began, they let their feelings known with a lot of noise.

It worked. It was 22–0 in the Aviator's favor when the last score came on a rare and very exciting play. The Aviators blocked a Glenville punt deep in their territory, Jim Davidson got contact on the ball and defensive end Paul Trieff caught it in midair in the end zone—a touchdown? Maybe, but Trieff, in the excitement of the moment, took off down the field toward his own goal! Alliance's Ernie Prince and Lee Woolf took off after him, yelling at him to stop; at the same time, a Glenville player was chasing him and finally knocked him down at the Glenville 30! One referee called a touchdown, but another one downfield signaled the ball down at the 30, so Alliance lined up to put the ball in play and Glenville got ready to defend, not at all unhappy at the turn of events. Coach Knowlton was frantically trying to get the official's attention that a touchdown had been signaled and finally did get the whistle. Play was stopped, and the officials huddled and ultimately called the play a touchdown for Alliance! Glenville then raised loud protestations. But that was it, 28–0, and for the rest of the game Alliance had its subs in to gain some experience.

On Tuesday, October 21, Marion Harding and its fans were rewarded with the terrific news that they were now ranked 4th in the Associated Press Poll, behind no. 1 Massillon, no. 2 Alliance and no. 3 Cleveland Cathedral Latin. The Prexies were the most offensively successful team in the Top 10, however, rolling up 210 points in their six wins. Cathedral Latin was second with 181 points and a 5-0-1 record. The Prexie defense was no. 8 out of the Top 10, having allowed only 48 points. Massillon was the beneficiary of a Warren Harding (the previous week's no. 1) loss to Canton Central Catholic by a score of 8–0. That loss moved Warren down to 5th place. Troy and Mansfield dropped out, and Elyria moved back in. Springfield was beaten by Hamilton, 8–6, and Newark beat Zanesville (its first defeat), 14–6. Youngstown East beat Rayen, 8–0. It was a crazy week!

A non-conference opponent was next on the list for Harding to entertain: the Ashland Arrows, a team with a strong and historic legacy in Ohio high school football. That was in the past, and Harding sent them home with a 56–14 traumatic defeat on their record.

Marion Harding started thinking about Fremont Ross, a team who had beaten them in 1957 and of whom a lot of lingering feelings of "what might have been" radiated throughout the Prexie locker room.

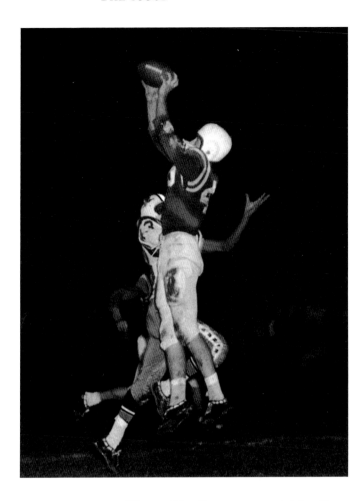

Roy Allen of Alliance makes a grab. *Courtesy Canton Repository.*

Elsewhere around the state, no. 5 Warren Harding upset no. 1 Massillon, 6–0!

Canton's Fawcett Stadium was the setting for the next big "game of the week" in Ohio on October 24. The Aviators of Alliance, unbeaten but with one tie and battling to stay at or near the top of the polls, traveled to the nexus of high school football to do battle with the legendary Canton McKinley Bulldogs.

The first three quarters of the game, however, were a weird mishmash of fumbles, interceptions and ineptness that was unlike either team up to that point; Bobby Brown, for instance, fumbled three times to the Bulldogs and had only 3 net yards! Inspired, the Bulldogs played very hard but just could not get a score, even though the breaks were going against Alliance and giving every chance to McKinley to take advantage of them. They just couldn't get it done; instead, it was the Aviators who finally broke through, and late in the game Alliance got it together and struggled through sheer grit to score twice, making the score 16–0.

They would take it. Walt Zingg passed well and directed the offense with skill and tenacity, keeping his guys looking forward and forgetting the first half. They knew they were going to win—it was just a matter of getting that first big play, and Brown provided it. The defense was praised mightily, having held the opponent scoreless for their third straight shutout and fourth of the season.

Alliance had sold a record number of tickets for an away game this week: 2,122 adults and 377 students, with many other Aviator fans buying their tickets in Canton. It was estimated that more than 3,000 out of the 11,000 total tickets purchased were Alliance supporters.

It was a different Fremont Little Giants team who were to welcome the Prexies to place this year. Last year, they were the Buckeye Conference champions and had whipped Harding, 24–0; this year they were 1-6, a win over Fostoria their only victory.

All signs pointed to a strong domination of the Little Giants by the Prexies in this game. To date, Harding had scored 266 points and given up only 62; in the conference, they had scored 90 and given away 36. A victory against Fremont would give Marion a share of the conference title, so a win was a must-have, both practically and emotionally. And it would be the first Fremont defeat for Harding's eleven since 1947.

Speaking of emotion, this week Harding climbed to no. 1 in the UPI Poll and to no. 3 in the Associated Press Poll, climbing past Cleveland Cathedral Latin for that spot and making banner headlines on the Marion Star's sports page. Harding had five 1st-place votes and Latin had nine, but Latin did not have enough 2nd- and 3rd-place votes to stay ahead of the Prexies. Harding still led all teams in the Top 10 in scoring. Alliance climbed to no. 1 in the AP via its win over Canton McKinley and Massillon Washington's loss to Warren Harding. The 7-0-1 Aviators pulled in 293 poll points to Warren's 286; forty-six sports editors voted on a 10-9-8-etc. basis.

Marion Harding had the only clean record in the AP Top 10 with zero losses and zero ties. If it continued, this '58 group would be Harding's only unbeaten and untied team in history, the 1939 and 1941 unbeaten teams incurring ties that marred their records. Coach Larson said on the day before the game, "We want this victory and we mean to get it. The boys are conscious that nothing short of a convincing victory will suffice."

Coach Knowlton. *Courtesy Canton Repository.*

A huge caravan of supporters geared up to make the trip to Fremont. It was October 31, 1958. With Harding's defense clicking, Fremont was held scoreless and it was 14–0 at the half. It was a harbinger of things to come.

The headlines in the *Marion Star* on Saturday, November 1, 1958, declared that Harding had broken a long-standing jinx and battered Fremont, 40–6. A picture showed about one thousand fans welcoming the Prexies back home at almost 1:30 a.m.

Harding had one last team to defeat: the Sandusky Blue Streaks, a team who were down on their luck this year but potentially lethal anytime they played the Marion Harding Presidents.

Alliance had Youngstown North up next, and like Fremont, it was a bad year; in fact, it hadn't won a game yet. The Aviators had a lot of desire against Youngstown North, for while Harding was whipping Fremont Ross, 40–6, Alliance put a total and complete hurt on Youngstown North, 40–0! It was the team's fourth consecutive shutout and fifth of the year, the highest point total of the season and Coach Knowlton's eighty-fourth victory as the Alliance high school football coach.

It was quiet in the locker room after the game. Coach Knowlton was not satisfied with the way the Aviators played and knew they were capable of much more. They would get their chance against Akron Hower the following week, a team Knowlton told them would be much tougher than the one they played that night. Uh-huh.

For Marion Harding's last game of the 1958 season, more than 3,200 advance tickets had been sold, and additional bleachers were being set up for the overflow crowd that was expected. Harding principal Darl Gatchall said it was the most advanced number of tickets he had seen sold since he could remember. Coach Larson said it for everyone when he was quoted as saying, "A defeat will make us just another football team." In the back of his mind was the fact that all the Top 10 had suffered a defeat or a tie except for Harding and now Dayton Fairmont.

For the ninth straight time, Harding won the toss and elected to go on offense. Starting at the 23, the Presidents went down the field in seventeen plays, making first downs when it was fourth down and short, with Tommy Pritchard getting one of them by sneaking over center and Pete Porietis busting for 17. Getting down close, Rocky Evans got the TD. On this drive, Abner Thomas preserved the forward progress by falling on a fumble and keeping it from the Blue Streaks. It was 12–0 at the half, and Harding ended up winning the game.

As the gun was sounded, the players grabbed Coach Gordon Larson and carried him off the field. Cars were waiting, and the players and coaches were chauffeured to the Marion County Courthouse in downtown Marion, where Mayor Wendell Strong and School Superintendent Robert S. Brown proclaimed the Prexies state champions. There were two weeks left and many important games to be played, but the Presidents were no. 1 in the UPI and no. 2 in the AP, with the Alliance Aviators holding the top spot there. Anything could happen, but for Harding, the unbeaten and untied season was an astounding achievement, and no one was going to tell them different! The final standings would be released on November 18. In the meantime, the city of Marion would celebrate heartily.

On Tuesday, November 4, 1958, an election day, the writers who voted for the AP high school football poll voted this way:

	AP	Points	Record
1	Alliance	304	7-0-1
2	Marion Harding	270	8-0-0
3	Cleveland Cathedral Latin	240	7-0-1
4	Massillon	204	6-1-1
5	Newark	118	7-0-1
6	Springfield	116	7-1-0
7	Elyria	101	7-1-0
8	Dayton Fairmont	81	8-0-0
9	Portsmouth	74	7-1
10	Toledo Central Catholic	72	6-1-1

Marion Harding was the prolific Top 10 scoring machine with 306 points while giving up only 68. Elyria was second in scoring with 249 points while giving up 56. Alliance had 192 to date while giving up 34. Clearly the top two schools were defined for their offense (Harding) and defense (Alliance) just looking at these statistics. But we know that isn't totally true, as both teams had superior athletes and most played both ways. It was just a matter in some of these games which way the ball bounced and the opportunities they got.

At the Alliance Booster Club meeting that week, Coach Knowlton told the listeners that their opponent, Akron Hower, was much bigger and stronger than his team and if they use that strength well they will give the Aviators all they can handle. He needn't have worried. The Aviators won 76–0! It was the same the following week against East Liverpool, with Alliance knocking that team out 52–0.

What a year this had been for the people of Marion and Alliance. Both teams moving up the polls week by week, game by game; players making huge plays when they needed them; the fans supporting them by traveling to every away game in large numbers; and the cities promoting them like presidential candidates. It must have been a very heady experience for these young men. Both towns were blue-collar communities with a manufacturing base; people had lived there for many years and invested time and sweat into making both places a great place to live—and the activities after each school won their state championship recognition bore that out.

Up in Alliance, the town went as crazy as Marion after the Aviators whipped East Liverpool. After the game, Superintendent of Schools

Granville S. Hammond and Mayor Dave Mainwaring claimed the state football championship as their own in front of a raucous crowd of noisy fans. The next day, the *Alliance Review* went with a big, bold black font on its front page that read, "Unbeaten Aviators Hailed as State Champions." The 9-0-1 season was the first since 1932 for Alliance. Also, that day, the team and its boosters were feted at the American Legion hall, where Coach Knowlton spoke of the season as a complete team effort.

Enduring torrential rain all week, some the heaviest in many years, and waiting on a snowstorm to strike from Canada that had left ten people dead, the town celebrated like it was eighty degrees! Coach Knowlton said in a 1977 interview, "Well we came back into the city, we had a police escort and I don't think I've ever seen the City of Alliance behind anything like they were that particular night. We had quite a celebration which lasted 'til the wee hours of the morning and everybody it seemed that everyone in Alliance was at the celebration. People were very happy for the football squad and I'm sure the football players were too. I know they, the players, talk about that even to this day about the way people were behind them when they came back into town that night."

The city council passed a resolution noting the achievements of the Alliance High School football team. Mayor Mainwaring proclaimed November 18 as Champion Day, and the students took that occasion to parade through the streets to the public square after a giant rally at the school auditorium (the players were on fire trucks and other kinds of flatbed vehicles). A large cake decorated as a football field was donated by Eagle Bakery in Alliance and was scripted with "Congratulations State Champs" and "Aviators—1958." Mainwaring gave the key to the city to Coach Knowlton. The players were brought out individually, and the crowd roared for each one, shaking the rafters of the building. The rally ended with the playing of the alma mater by the high school band, directed by Eric Duro.

Many had learned the night before that the Associated Press had voted the Aviators no. 1, with Marion Harding at no. 2, and would receive the Rutgers University Hall of Fame Trophy in recognition of gaining the AP's top spot, a trophy that goes to that team permanently if won three times.

But the United Press International Coaches Poll thought differently, showing Alliance at no. 2 behind no. 1 Marion Harding. The *Alliance Review*, in analyzing the polls, noted that the Aviators finished only six points behind the Prexies in the UPI and attributed that to geography in

Coach Knowlton receives the Rutgers University Hall of Fame Trophy for the AP top spot. *Courtesy Canton Repository.*

part, as the UPI serviced more newspapers in areas from which Marion would be likely to draw votes. It thought that the six-point margin validated the impression Alliance made around the state.

The final polls looked like this:

AP	Points	Record	UPI	Points	Record
Alliance (15)	389	9-0-1	Marion Harding (9)	230	9-0-0
Marion Harding (7)	319	9-0	Alliance (8)	224	9-0-1
Springfield (6)	243	8-0-1	Cleveland Cathedral Latin (1)	149	8-0-1
Massillon Washington (2)	230	8-1-1	Massillon Washington (3)	137	8-1-1

AP	Points	Record	UPI	Points	Record
Cleveland Cathedral Latin (6)	227	8-0-1	Springfield (1)	133	9-1-0
Elyria	132	8-0-1	Elyria	75	8-1-0
Dayton Fairmont (2)	108	9-0-0	Dayton Fairmont (1)	65	9-0-0
Toledo DeVilbiss	94	8-0-2	Cincy Roger Bacon (2)	61	10-0-0
Youngstown East (3)	87	9-0-1	Parma	48	9-0-0
Toledo Libby (5)	78	8-0-1	Warren Harding (1)	39	7-2-1

Who was the true state champion in 1958? We had then two bodies voting, and like today, no one sees all the teams play. Like today, the voters were influenced by highlights they read (today it is mostly television/internet clips) and word of mouth. Other influences came to the fore, such as biases, prejudices and relationships. Is it and was it fair? Well, it was what we had then, and it worked for the most part, except this time. The two polls did not agree, and thus there was a split championship. Alliance might say that the AP means more because of the Rutgers Trophy, and Marion might say the UPI is voted on by coaches who know more about football than writers do. The Associated Press, comprised that year of fifty-one sports writers (thirty-four from newspapers and seventeen from radio-television stations) voted Alliance no. 1, probably based on its tie with Massillon. But was Massillon really that tough that season, or was it riding the crest of a wave built up over the years? Alliance beat Canton McKinley, but the Bulldogs were nowhere to be found in the polls at season's end.

Marion Harding beat Elyria, a quality team who finished 6th in the both polls and was the Pioneers' only loss of the season. In the AP, Youngstown East finished 9th with three 1st-place votes, but in the UPI, it was not even in the Top 25, finishing with just five points in the voting! Two Toledo teams were in the AP Top 10 but not in the UPI Top 10! The top seven teams in both polls were the same, but in different spots, and after that they were all over the place. Cincinnati Roger Bacon was 8th in the UPI Poll but garnered only forty-three points in the Associated Press Poll.

As for some of the personalities, you look at Gordon Larson and Mel Knowlton and you see so many similarities that it's eerie. Both were taskmasters and structured their practices to be hard, fast and timely—no wasted motion or time. Both knew the game quite well and hired excellent assistant coaches. They could motivate the players without violence or instilling fear and during the game were masters of feeling how things were going—putting the right guys in at the right time and calling the right plays.

Coach Larson

Coach Larson won UPI's and AP's Ohio Coach of the Year honors for his 1958 accomplishment and would be the first to say that he owed everything to the players and his assistants. He coached the North All-Stars in the North-South game in 1959. In his four years at Marion Harding, he was 25-9-2.

Coach Larson spent two years working for Woody Hayes and then accepted the head coaching position at the University of Akron. He was there twelve seasons (1961–72) and left with a 74-33-5 mark, including seasons of 7-2 (1968), 9-1 ('69), 7-3 ('70) and 8-2 ('71)—his .683 winning percentage is the best in Akron's history. His 1968 team established a new milestone by becoming the first Akron team to play in a postseason game, the Grantland Rice Bowl. A native of that city, Larson had played basketball at South High with Ara Parseghian, the future Notre Dame coach, and graduated from Kent State in 1949.

Coach Larson was named the athletic director at the University of Akron in 1970 and served in that capacity until his retirement in 1985. As athletic director, he guided the Zips from the NCAA College Division to NCAA Division II and, ultimately, to NCAA Division I status. A memorial fund in his name was established at the university in 2005 by family and friends for a freshman football player who was a person of integrity and one who could be trusted to uphold the Larson legacy. The Zips head football coach has full authority in selecting the recipient. Coach Larson is in the Ohio Football Coaches Hall of Fame. What a guy!

Coach Knowlton

Equally, Mel Knowlton was inducted into the Ohio High School Football Coaches Hall of Fame after compiling a twenty-four-year record of 150-85-8. Like Larson, he had been named Ohio Coach of the Year in 1954 (as with Larson, taking no personal credit and giving it all to his players and coaches) and was twice selected as Stark County Coach of the Year (1958 being one of them). After retiring from coaching, he remained as athletic director at Alliance until 1978. He was inducted into the Miami University Hall of Fame in 1981. He had earned three letters each in baseball and basketball and was named All-Conference in both sports at Miami University. He had participated in football for two years as a player and served as a student assistant with the freshman football team for two years. He was also a member of the Athletic Board of Control. After graduation, he returned to Massillon, where he coached under his high school mentor, Paul Brown.

When asked in 1977 why he did not take one of the numerous offers to go to a college team or larger school, he said, "Some of them I didn't think that the possibilities were there for doing the kind of job that everybody was hoping would be done. And then with some of the others I felt, that I had been in Alliance for a long time—I liked the people, I liked the players and the life, and they were continually willing to fight to get the job done, and I think it was a combination of those two things which made me stay here." Those opportunities included, but were probably not limited to, Marshall University, Vanderbilt, Annapolis, University of Oregon and Purdue.

Coach Knowlton had an impact on every young man he coached, including stars such as Pro Football Hall of Famer Len Dawson, who said at Canton, "As you know, I'm from Alliance, Ohio, just down the road, where [Coach] Mel Knowlton started me on my way to becoming a football player, and an accomplished one, because he taught me the fundamentals necessary to play the game. I will be forever grateful to Mel Knowlton."

The Players

For Marion Harding, Bob Middleton, Rocky Evans, Mike Chamberlain, Gary Massie and Pete Sykes made All-Ohio squads, and Middleton was proclaimed Lineman of the Year in both polls. Pete Porietis and John Lawson were granted Honorable Mention All-Ohio status. Middleton and Evans were both Honorable Mention All-Americans. The team gained 3,152 yards and held opponents to 1,533 yards. Rocky Evans was the team's leading scorer in this 1958 season. Pete Porietis went on to his senior year of 1959 and continued with his stellar performances. He holds the Marion Harding records for most touchdowns scored by a running back; total scoring, with 252 points; single-game scoring with 56 points against Fremont Ross in 1959, as well as getting eight touchdowns in that game; and finishing 1959 with 1,080 yards rushing, one of the best years and careers a Harding running back ever had.

Bob Middleton was perhaps one of the greatest football players and athletes to graduate from Marion Harding High School. He was a three-sport star, playing three seasons of varsity basketball and still in the Top 10 in scoring with 674 total points. He was on the track team as a weight man; his discus throw of 184 feet, 6 inches on April 25, 1959, at the Ohio Wesleyan Relays in Delaware (beating the recognized national high school record, which was then 184 feet, 2.5 inches) reigns still as one of the most significant track events in United States track history; and, of course, he played both ways on the football team. Harding's 480-yard alternate hurdle relay team broke a school record by running third in the event with a heretofore unheard-of 58.2 seconds. Footballers John Lawson, Pete Porietis and Middleton joined Ted Jolliff on this team.

Middleton went to Ohio State to play for Woody Hayes and there played with greats such as Bob Ferguson, Tom Matte and Bob Vogel. He was the 180th NFL pick by the Buffalo Bills in the 1963 NFL draft and later coached football and tennis at Ohio Northern University in Ada, Ohio. Bob Middleton could do it all and remains one of the most talked-about and fondly remembered stars the Prexies ever produced.

Walt Zingg was named MVP of Stark County, only the third such time an Alliance player had been so named, the others being John Borton and Len Dawson. We know about Dawson, but Borton was another great Aviator quarterback who was twice All-Ohio in 1949 and 1950 and played at Ohio State, where he received All-American honors as well. He was in the military for three years following college and tried for a brief time to make the Cleveland Browns but gave up because of an elbow injury and because his skills had rusted too much. Walter made first-team All-Ohio at QB in the AP selection.

Roy Allen and Bobby Brown were named to the first-team All–Stark County team, and Bill Coldsnow was named to the second team. Allen, Coldsnow, Tom Baddley and Bobby Brown were AP Honorable Mention All-Ohioans.

1959

In 1959, the Massillon Tigers reclaimed the state championship under Coach Leo Strang. Leo's team just steamrolled over everyone in 1959, their closest victory a 36–18 win over Akron Garfield. They put up five shutouts, including a 70–0 thumping of Mansfield Senior and a 20–0 season-ending overthrow of Canton McKinley. The *Canton Repository*'s Charlie Powell said of this game, "The Tigers did no extraordinary things, they simply did the ordinary thing extraordinarily well." Well said.

The Tigers of Massillon Washington ended the middle decade of the twentieth century with a record of 82-7-2 for a 91.11 percent winning percentage. This decade saw the Tigers win six Ohio state championships as voted by the Associated Press and four mythical national championships. They were ranked at or near the top each year, and the lowest they were ever ranked in this decade was no. 8 in 1956, when they were merely 8-2.

Marion Harding: Postscript to a Championship, 1959

Coming off a championship year, winning the tough Buckeye Conference and then the UPI state crown in a hotly and fiercely debated week-to-week contest with Alliance, the Presidents were primed to go for the repeat. They had lost some great players, like Bob Middleton and Rocky Evans, but also had a solid nucleus of skillful vets who would be back to step up, led by co-captains Tom Pritchard and Clyde Thomas, as well as guys like Ed Schoonmaker, Don Kern and Gerald Bosh. Pete Porietis was back as well, one of the best running backs to put on the red and black of Marion Harding and arguably the best, many in Marion would tell you.

Coach Gordon Larson was gone too, last year's coach of the Presidents who took them to an undefeated record and the state title, winning the Coach of the Year Award in the process and getting hired by Woody Hayes at Ohio State. Pretty good results! Pete Risen took his place. Their only loss was a heartbreaker to powerful Elyria, and they finished behind Fairmont and Springfield, as well as champ Massillon.

Salem High School Makes a Run Under Coach Earle Bruce

Zadok Street and John Straughan (pronounced "strawn") founded Salem, Ohio, in 1806. Named after Salem, New Jersey, where Zadok Street was from, Salem comes from the name Jerusalem, which means "city of peace." Salem, Ohio, was critical in the American Underground Railroad and in 1850 hosted the first Women's Rights Convention in Ohio, the second such convention in the United States after Seneca Falls, New York, hosted one in 1848.

Salem High School athletes are called the Quakers, after the many settlers who moved there. In 1959, the Salem Quakers were anything but peaceful.

Notable about the Quakers this year is that it was the last of a four-year run coached by a man named Earle Bruce. Coach Bruce had matriculated at Ohio State University in 1953, and Salem was his first head coaching job. He was only twenty-four years old. Leaving for a larger school after this fourth season, he was 28-9 and left with the best winning percentage of any football coach coming through the school at .757.

In 1959, there were some new names in the Top 10, not just Salem but also Marietta, Fairmont, Parma and Canton Central Catholic up there with Massillon, Elyria and Marion Harding. At 8-1 and securing seven shutouts, the Salem Quakers were just as special as these other teams. One great story was tackle Ned Chappell becoming the first Salem football player to play in the annual Ohio North-South football game in Canton's Fawcett Stadium.

Coach Bruce built the program over his four years there into a contender and launched his own meteoric career. His previous two years had him going 9-1 and 7-2. You will read more about Coach Bruce's career during the next few years before he went to Ohio State. Do Sandusky and Massillon sound familiar?

Salem	42	Cleveland Lincoln	0
Salem	48	Ravenna	0
Salem	32	Canton Timken	0
Salem	0	Ambridge, Pa.	14
Salem	6	Akron Hoban	0
Salem	50	Wellsville	0
Salem	36	Boardman	8
Salem	20	East Liverpool	0
Salem	58	Girard	0

Marietta, Ohio, is the county seat of Washington County, Ohio. Marietta is in southeastern Ohio at the mouth of the Muskingum River and its junction with the Ohio River. It is home to Marietta College, a DIII liberal arts college that has a rich history in both academics and sports. Its baseball program has won many national championships and sent many players on to the majors. The high school football team has been notable for some time, and it, too, has had its share of tough footballers going on to college and pro careers.

In 1959, the Tigers were part of the Central Ohio League (COL) and went undefeated with a 10-0 record, finishing 6th in the AP rankings. This great season was a response to 1958, when they lost their first two games but then reeled off six wins in a row.

They felt confident they could do much better in 1959. And they did, averaging thirty-five points and 300 yards of total offense per game. The defense allowed the opposition an average of only nine points per contest. In 1959, the Tigers outrushed opponents 2,550 to 881 yards, contributing to four shutouts. Several All-Ohioans came from this team, including Jim Farley, Neil Gregory, Phil Offenberger and Frank Christie. Dick Wendelkin gained 818 yards rushing this year for an 8.6

Marietta High School's 1959 undefeated team. *Courtesy Bob Fogle.*

Three MHS players receiving pictures that had once hung in the Marietta High School gym lobby. They originally hung pictures of All-Americans and modified that to include All-Ohio athletes. These three have all been inducted into the MHS Athletic Hall of Fame. *Left to right*: Jim Farley, Neil Gregory and Bob Fogle. All played on the 1959 undefeated football team. Ah to be the age of the guys in the pictures again! *Courtesy Bob Fogle.*

average. Three backs averaged more than 7 yards per carry. Christie, the quarterback, averaged only eight passes per game but 30 yards per completion. Phil Offenberger was the defensive quarterback in the mold of Dick Butkus, Lawrence Taylor or Luke Kuechly in today's world, according to teammate Bob Fogle. Reportedly, fifty-car caravans to away games were the norm.

The Tigers' last game of the season was against Newark on a Friday the thirteenth, and they won, 14–0, playing in front of five thousand "hysterical fans," according to *Marietta Times* sportswriter Bill Robinson.

In this last game, Marietta only threw three passes, completing none. The team grounded it out with 207 yards rushing. The Tigers scored in each of the first two quarters and held Newark the rest of the way, even stopping their opponent when they got down to Marietta's 3-yard line. They were not to be denied this night! It was a Hollywood ending, a perfect ending that all high school footballers dream about. Yes, it had happened before and since. But to Marietta that night, it was their ending, their dream come true. Just the way they wanted it.

The Tigers of Marietta had great seasons before this and would achieve future success as well, but this 1959 team is one of those they still talk about around this small industrial town close to two ancient flowing rivers.

Parma Senior High School Redmen

Originally surveyed in 1806 and known as Greenbriar back then, Parma became a city in 1931, and by the 1950s, it had become one of the nation's fastest-growing cities. Today, it is the seventh-largest city in Ohio and second in Cuyahoga County after Cleveland.

Establishing a team in 1926, Parma High School did not have a real field to play on, so later in 1928, the team captain, Lee Bailey, oversaw the team as they cleared an area behind the first Parma High School of fruit trees and planted some grass. This became their home field. In 1953, that field become Byers Field, which is the current 11,200 seat Parma Byers Field Stadium, the second-largest stadium in Cuyahoga County after Cleveland's Municipal Stadium, home of the NFL Browns.

Doug Lyons was a two-sport standout at Parma High, lettering twice in both football and basketball. He was a key member of the Redmen LEL Championship football teams of 1958 and 1959. These teams won nineteen consecutive games and enjoyed two undefeated seasons. Lyons was selected as both team MVP and Lake Erie League MVP in 1959. He was also recognized by the local media, being selected for both the Cleveland Press All-Scholastic team and the *Cleveland Plain Dealer*'s "Dream Team." He earned honorable mention All-Ohio honors and was selected to play in the North-South All-Star football game. Lyons played football at The Ohio State University and was a member of the 1961 NCAA National Championship Buckeye team.

Arnie Chonko, a key member on the 1959 team, also played baseball and basketball as well for the Redmen. He was a two-time All–Lake Erie League and two-time All-District selection in baseball and a three-time All-LEL honoree in football.

Arnie was selected as the LEL MVP and the Cleveland Touchdown Club Player of the Year in football in 1960, as well as earning All-Ohio

Above: The 1958 Parma Senior High 9-0 team, ranked no. 9 in the AP Poll. *Courtesy Parma Senior High School.*

Left: Doug Lyons, *center*, at Ohio State University. *Courtesy Parma Senior High School.*

Arnold "Arnie" Chonko of Parma High School. *Courtesy Parma Senior High School.*

honors in both football and baseball. Arnie received three letters in baseball and three letters in football while attending The Ohio State University. In baseball, he was a two-time All–Big Ten selection and an NCAA All-American.

In football, Arnie was a three-year starting defensive back for the Buckeyes, earning both All–Big Ten and NCAA All-American honors in 1964. He played in the 1965 East-West Shrine Game. Arnie was a two-time All-Academic Big Ten and won two-time Academic All-American honors. He was later named to the Ohio State All-Century team in both football and baseball and was elected to the OSU Athletic Hall of Fame.

Eschewing professional sports, he attended Ohio State's medical school and is today a respected doctor at the University of Kansas Medical Center. Today, there is a Chonko Scholar-Athlete Award at Parma High School awarded in his honor.

1959 OHIO AP STATE POLL

1. Massillon (10-0) (also National Champion)
2. Springfield (10-0)
3. Fairmont (9-0)
4. Marion Harding (8-1)
5. Toledo DeVilbiss (8-0-1)
6. Marietta (9-0)
7. Canton Central (9-1)
8. Salem (8-1)
9. Parma (9-0)
10. Elyria (7-1-1)

THE 1960s

1960

The Massillon Washington Tigers—under the leadership of Coach Leo Strang, co-captains Virgil Buktus and Martin Gugov and All-Ohioans Art Hastings and Lawson Black—ended the 1960 season 10-1, their sole setback a loss at Warren Harding, 19–18. Penalties, mistakes in execution, a player ejection and any other what-ifs you can imagine were all instrumental in Warren beating the Tigers. But Warren didn't care—they had beaten Massillon!

Massillon versus Canton McKinley on November 19, 1960. *Courtesy Canton McKinley High School.*

When the clock wound down, chaos erupted with the fans storming the field and the band playing loudly (rocking it long after the crowd had left). It was a great win for the Warren team but a tough loss for the Tigers as they sat tearful in their silent locker room. It was their first loss after twenty straight wins. Would it affect their chances at another state crown? As it turned out, it didn't. Massillon was voted another title.

Dayton Colonel White Cougars

One of the better stories this year, though, was that of the Dayton Colonel White Cougars, a new, just four-year-old high school in Dayton that had spun off from Fairview. The school had started that first year, fielding football with all underclassmen under Coach Jim Eby and had done well, culminating in 1960 with an undefeated season and being ranked 5th in the AP Poll at the end of the year.

Dayton at this time was growing with Wright-Patterson Air Force Base, a hub around which countless industries abounded. There were some good football schools in the Miami Valley region in the southwestern part of the state, and to become so successful so quickly was extraordinary. As Colonel White was coming into its biggest game that year against Dayton Chaminade, a team who had won the city crown sixteen of the past twenty seasons, the routes to the game were jammed with traffic, ending up as a standing room–only crowd. Chaminade was 7-2 that year but had tough kids who thrived in big games. They had also beat Colonel White in 1959, 23–16.

Colonel White was a close-knit team, as many of the players were of longtime Jewish and Greek families who had grown up together. The strength that comes from knowing your teammates well, depending on one another and supporting them through sweltering practices paid off in this game. Highly motivated this night, they whipped Chaminade, 32–12, for the Dayton City League Championship.

Today, Colonel White is no more, having merged with another school, and is now called Thurgood Marshall High School.

Port Clinton High Redskins

The Port Clinton High Redskins are in Port Clinton, Ohio, on the shores of Lake Erie, the town being the county seat of Ottawa County. It is a little more than forty miles east of Toledo and is a busy tourist destination, with many parks and festivals in the area drawing hundreds of thousands annually. It is known as the Walleye Capital of the World.

The team's coach in 1960, Joe Lukac, had graduated from Port Clinton High in 1940 and then served in the U.S. Army Air Corps for three years. He attended Ohio State for one year and Bowling Green for three, where he played football and was on BGSU's 1948 undefeated team. He became the head football and track coach for the Redskins in 1951.

In 1960, the Redskins powered through all those who dared to line up against them and went unbeaten and untied, finishing 10th in the final AP Poll of the season. Coach Lukac would spend twenty years as the head coach of both football and track and became a vital part of the community in later life. In track, he went ten straight years without losing a dual meet. This year, he would lead the team to a 10-0 record and go undefeated again in 1962 by going 9-0-1, finishing 17th in the AP Poll.

Like many coaches, Coach Lukac made a lasting impression on his charges. One I spoke to and e-mailed with was Milt Long, a sophomore on this 10-0 team who had not played football until this year but had yearned to, as he resided outside the town and transportation into town for practices was challenging because of his parents' jobs. He told me, "Football was just what guys did in Port Clinton." He also noted, "Several times games were well in hand, so Coach Joe Lukac cleared the bench. The seniors that year were awesome!" Milt went on to start at middle guard his junior year until getting hurt halfway into the season. He started at center and inside linebacker his senior year, when the Redskins went 9-0-1.

Matriculating at Hobart College in Geneva, New York, Milt played all four years as a running back and linebacker while working to pay his college costs. He went to the Navy Officer Candidate School in Newport, Rhode Island, and later served as a surface line officer with deployments to the Mediterranean and Indian Oceans. After his navy service, Milt started a defense contracting company that he later sold after a twenty-year run to manage his assets, including a small family farm just a few miles outside Port Clinton.

Milt said the town was totally behind the football team, and on Friday nights, the main shopping street was deserted, when normally it would be crowded with shoppers. After home games, the kids would gather at Phil's Inn, even though 3.2 beer was still beyond them. The first event on Saturday morning was to go get the *Toledo Blade* to see how their game was covered and how other teams in the area fared.

According to Milt, Coach Joe Lukac was a head coach who drove the kids to be the best team they could be by practicing, practicing and practicing some more. Two-a-days in August and then after school until lights were needed to continue the session were normal. Mental toughness and physical courage were needed to play for Coach Joe. For years, Milt said he had a small picture of Coach Joe tacked to a bulletin board to remind him that life's challenges needed the intensity and focus the team learned playing football in Port Clinton. His lessons were no small part of Milt's success later in life. He remained grateful to have had his guidance while growing up. He said there were a few very tense moments on the bridge of a navy destroyer when Milt conjured up a little extra courage by listening in his head to the Port Clinton High School fight song.

Lastly, Milt left me with an observation that I think every Ohio high school footballer shares. He said, "If you grew up in Ohio and particularly if you played football in Ohio, you have an identity that has meaning beyond the scope of what I will write today. For very good reasons, when I was the owner of a small defense contracting firm, I knew who was from Ohio, and a bond was formed among us. You need a few good Buckeyes to succeed in any organization."

Sandusky High School Blue Streaks

In 1960, there began an era at Sandusky High School called the "Fabulous '60s." Led by new coach Earle Bruce, the Blue Streaks would create an unparalleled decades-long record that any school and community would be proud of. You will read more about this amazing run in the stories to come.

1960 OHIO AP FINAL POLL
1. Massillon (10-1) (also 7th in national poll)—defeated Alliance; lost to Warren Harding
2. Niles McKinley (9-0-1)
3. Alliance (9-2) lost to Massillon, Niles
4. Sandusky (9-1)
5. Dayton Colonel White (10-0)
6. Cincinnati Purcell (9-0)
7. Marion Harding (7-1-1)
8. Toledo Central (9-1)
9. Troy (9-1)
10. Port Clinton (10-0)

1961

The Niles McKinley Dragons' home is in Niles, Ohio, up in Trumbull County over by the Pennsylvania border in northeast Ohio. It has played the game since 1912, the area having been settled in 1800.

As Coach Tony Mason's footballers prepared that summer of '61 for the upcoming campaign, they were thinking about unfinished business from the year before. Ending the year at 9-0-1 and a second-place finish to Massillon Washington in the 1960 AP Poll left a bitter taste in their mouths. They were determined to rectify matters. In fact, they beat Massillon, 12–0, in a September 4 scrimmage watched by an estimated five thousand fans to set the tone for the year.

Confidence gained, they opened-up to a standing room–only crowd by whipping East Liverpool, 40–0. They blitzed through the rest of the schedule, getting to a 9-0 record to set up a showdown with the Alliance Aviators, who at this point were ranked 3rd in the AP Poll with an 8-1 record, losing only to Massillon. The Red Dragons were ranked 2nd.

It was what the Red Dragons had been waiting for, and they did not disappoint their supporters as they slaughtered the Aviators, 30–6, in front of eight thousand fans. Concurrently, Massillon barely squeaked by a 5-4 Parma team, 21–20, in Cleveland Municipal Stadium and then followed that performance up by beating a 6-3 Canton McKinley team by just 7–6.

In this amazing year, Niles McKinley outscored its opponents 450-48. Massillon was once again good and considered by many voters to be the best in the state. Cincinnati Roger Bacon suffered its first home loss in three years, 12-0 to the Tigers. This year's Massillon Washington team was the first in history to win 11 games in a season.

However, just as many others believed that the Niles McKinley Red Dragons were as deserving, if not more so, than the Tigers. This year, Niles finished no. 1 in the AP, while the Tigers finished 2nd in the AP but snagged it in the UPI.

One sterling example of the kids Coach Mason had on this team was Charlie Kines, a stud two-way star who would graduate in June 1962 and go on to play at Michigan as an offensive tackle, be selected All–Big Ten and play in a Rose Bowl. After graduation, he became an officer in the Marine Corps and fought in Vietnam, leading his men in vicious hand-to-hand action in which 142 NVA were killed; he was awarded the Silver Star and a Purple Heart. Kines retired from the Corps a few years later as a captain and died in August 2010.

Massillon versus Canton McKinley on November 18, 1961—Massillon prevailed, 7–6. *Courtesy Canton McKinley High School.*

Senior Rick Sygar led all scorers this season with twenty-five TDs, and junior Bo Rein made it in twelve times. Nine different players hauled in seventeen interceptions, with Sygar picking off nine of them. Sygar was Ohio's Back of the Year and played at Michigan like Kines.

Bo Rein, who played on these great Niles teams, became All-Ohio in both football and baseball and played both sports at Ohio State University, helping the Buckeyes win a College World Series and playing in the backfield for Woody Hayes. Bo went on to coach at multiple schools, but after accepting the head football coaching job at LSU, he died in a plane crash on January 10, 1980, before taking charge of the program.

The Red Dragons outgained opponents in total yardage 3,572-1,078 this season. They gained 3,086 rushing yards. A total of fifteen different players rushed for positive yards, while fourteen different players scored touchdowns.

This hard-hitting 1961 Niles McKinley team would be selected the best high school football team in Trumbull County in the twentieth century.

Martins Ferry High School Purple Raiders

Martins Ferry, Ohio, the oldest European settlement in Ohio, is located across the Ohio River from Wheeling, West Virginia, in the eastern part of the state.

The Purple Raiders have been playing football for a long time and have had an ongoing rivalry with Bellaire High School for 111 years, the seventh longest in Ohio and the eighty-second longest in the nation. Each year they play for the SPARKY (Sportsmanship, Participation, Achievement, Rivalry, Knowledge, Youth) Trophy. Only fourteen minutes away from each other, the two schools define "rivalry." Both schools have sent players on to the professional levels.

From 1958–59 to 1961–62, the Purple Raiders of Martins Ferry went undefeated. That's right, undefeated. The streak was from the last game of the 1958 season to the first game of the 1962 season—thirty-two games in all. Not many teams nationwide can claim a streak like that. All three teams won the Ohio Valley Athletic Conference Championship, and each team had a different starting quarterback leading them. That is not normal.

In Ohio high school football history, Martins Ferry, from 1907 to 2017, has totaled seven hundred wins. Part of that total, this thirty-two-game streak that encompassed three complete seasons, was the result of great coaching, hard practices and, most importantly, heart. This heart was in each kid and was a key to their success. Raised in a predominantly coal, iron and steel economic environment, many wanted to succeed beyond Belmont County and the mills. Football and other sports provided such an opportunity. Martins Ferry is a small community with a lot pride, so much it just seemed to bust out in whatever sport was played. Larry Duck was one of those kids from whom it busted out, a three-year member of the undefeated teams.

A three-year starter on those stupendous football teams, Duck also played basketball and threw the discus and shot. Playing both ways, he was extremely athletic and was above average in the classroom, earning a spot on the Senior Scholastic All-American Team. He was also named to the first-team All-Conference and All-Ohio teams. Oh yeah, he was also named Ohio's UPI Back of the Year. He later went to Memphis State and was a three-year starter and MVP of the team his senior year, playing in the Blue-Gray All-Star Game in Alabama. But with all this skill and notoriety, he decided to come back home, spending thirty years as a coach, teacher and athletic director at Martins Ferry High School. That's a lot of heart.

1. Niles (10-0)—defeated Alliance
2. Massillon (11-0) (also 1st in UPI State Poll; National Champion)—defeated Alliance, Cincinnati Roger Bacon
3. Bellevue (9-0)
4. Cincinnati Roger Bacon (9-1)
5. Martins Ferry (10-0)
6. Hamilton Garfield (9-1)
7. Fairmont (9-0-2)
8. Alliance (9-2)—lost to Niles, Massillon
9. Toledo Macomber (7-1-1)
10. Middletown (8-1-1)

1962

The following year, 1962, an outstanding Toledo Central Catholic squad made a run and was rewarded with both polls voting them no. 1. They had been out of the limelight for some time and returned that year with a vengeance. Sandusky finished fourth once more, but Massillon was not in the Top 10, having suffered a 6-5 roughing-up by the teams it encountered.

This was another interesting year in Ohio high school football. The Alliance Aviators were beaten in their first game of the season by Lima Senior, and by the time they were into their sixth week, they were in 1st place at 5-1 in the AP. They were followed by Niles, Sandusky, Warren Harding and Lorain Admiral King. Middletown, Steubenville, Toledo Central Catholic, Cincinnati Roger Bacon and Springfield South brought up the bottom 5. The UPI ranked Niles no. 1 with Alliance no. 2, followed by Warren Harding, Sandusky, Lorain Admiral King, Cincinnati Roger Bacon, Steubenville, Middletown, Toledo Central Catholic and Fremont Ross. Niles followed Alliance in the AP by twenty-one points and led the Aviators in the UPI by just two points that week.

The following week, Niles gained some ground on the Aviators, trailing now by only fourteen points in the AP. Toledo Central Catholic leaped from 8th to 5th place, getting an additional eleven points. Cleveland St. Ignatius came in at 11th but got five 1st-place votes! Fremont Ross, the winner over Massillon Washington in its first game of the season, was getting set to clash with Lorain Admiral King. Other critical games coming up were Toledo

Central Catholic preparing for a titanic game with Steubenville (no. 8) on November 2, while the Niles team probably had their November 9 game with Alliance hovering around inside their heads.

Lorain Admiral King (named in honor of Fleet Admiral Ernest J. King, the chief of naval operations (CNO) of the United States Navy during World War II) won its game against Massillon Washington, and then Toledo Central Catholic took the field against the Steubenville Big Red the following week and came out victorious, 20–12, in a tough, hard-hitting battle. Lorain that week beat Marion Harding, 44–6; Sandusky tied Elyria, 20–20; and Middletown beat Richmond, Indiana, whose team was in that state's Top 5. Alliance was beaten by Toledo DeVilbiss in a game that made headlines in the sports pages along with Central Catholic's win. Niles beat a 3-4 Youngstown Chaney team in a squeaker by the score of 14–8.

The following week, Toledo Central Catholic was voted no. 1 in the AP and remained in that spot in the UPI. Even though Coach Tony Mason's Niles McKinley Red Dragons team had won their thirty-sixth game in a row, the AP voters saw Central Catholic's victory as deserving of the leap over the Dragons. The Fighting Irish from Toledo led the voting, 325 to Niles's 285, with 1st-place votes coming in at nineteen to five. They were followed that week in the AP by Lorain Admiral King, Warren Harding, Middletown, Toledo DeVilbiss, Roger Bacon, Sandusky, Steubenville and then Cleveland St. Ignatius in the no. 10 position. Coach Hoyman of Steubenville said that as far as he was concerned, "We lost to the state champions. And to date we are the second best." Circleville, having won its fourteenth in a row, was a quiet no. 11.

Niles McKinley played Alliance in a blockbuster game, and the two contenders had to sadly walk away with a 12–12 tie, although Niles must have felt worst because the team missed conversion attempts that contributed to the outcome.

The final AP Poll for 1962 showed the voters overwhelmingly in support of the 9-0 Toledo Central Catholic team as champions. Their vote total of 524 points (thirty-three 1st-place votes) was 187 more than runner-up 9-0-1 Warren Harding (ten 1st-place votes), coached by Ben Wilson. Since the first polls many weeks before, shifts had occurred: 8-0-1 Niles finished at no. 3, followed by 8-0-2 Sandusky, 9-1 Middletown, 8-1 Toledo DeVilbiss, 9-1 Steubenville, 9-0 Cincinnati Roger Bacon, 8-0 Cleveland St. Ignatius and, still in the Top 10 at 7-2-1, the Alliance Aviators. Undefeated Circleville with fifteen straight victories and winning its last game, 35–0, over Marion Franklin finished at no. 11, getting two 1st-place votes in the process!

1962 OHIO AP STATE POLL
1. Toledo Central Catholic (9-0)
2. Warren Harding (9-0-1)
3. Niles (8-0-1)—tied Alliance
4. Sandusky (8-0-2)
5. Middletown (9-1)
6. Toledo DeVilbiss (8-1)—defeated Alliance
7. Steubenville (9-1)
8. Cincinnati Roger Bacon (9-0)
9. Cleveland St. Ignatius (8-0)
10. Alliance (7-2-1)—tied Niles; lost to Lima Senior, Toledo DeVilbiss

Ten players from the 1962 Toledo Central Catholic team went on to play Division I football, including all four members of their offensive backfield.

Wyoming High School: A Singular 1960s Story

Wyoming High School is in Wyoming, Ohio, down in Hamilton County in the southwestern corner of the state. Wyoming began as a kind of a "bedroom" community for workers in neighboring areas, and it wasn't until the railroad went through that businesses began to call Wyoming proper their home. Right before the Civil War, the village was named Wyoming, and it wasn't until 1949 that it officially became a town.

The Wyoming school system is outstanding and usually ranked among the best in the state and nationwide. Five students from the class of 1885 were the first to graduate from Wyoming High School, and many thousands have since done the same. The school started playing football in 1919, and up through the 1940s, it did not suffer a losing season, its worst season coming in at 5-4-1 in 1939. The 1940s started off similarly, going 5-2-1, and then, in an amazing show of football prowess, the team went undefeated, untied and unscored on (182–0 in points) in 1941! That season set them in a class by themselves, for just a handful of teams in Ohio and America have achieved such perfection.

The years following that record book season were tough ones. The war was on, and the nucleus for good teams was sometimes hard to come by. The Cowboys had consecutive losing seasons up until 1948, when they got back on track to the tune of 6-2 and then went 8-1 in 1949. The first half of the

1950s were mediocre ones, 7-1-1 in 1950, 5-2-1 in 1952 and 6-3 in 1954. It was not until 1956 that the Cowboys would start to put together a string of winning seasons lasting twenty-three years that would be due, primarily, to one man: Coach Bob Lewis.

Lewis was a Portsmouth High grad and a graduate of Ohio Wesleyan University in Delaware, Ohio, served in the navy and then coached at Marysville High School before moving on to Wyoming. Reportedly, he was on his way to a Cincinnati Reds baseball game when he stopped by the school for an interview! Lewis brought with him a penchant for hard work, paying attention to details and discipline. With those traits well in hand, he took the Cowboys to new heights of achievement. Having gone 1-6-2 in 1955, Lewis got an 8-2 season out of them his first year in 1956, a significant turnaround. The next few years in the Lewis stimulation package looked like this:

1957	7-1-1
1958	9-0
1959	9-0
1960	8-0-2
1961	8-1-1

Coach Lewis entered the 1962 season with a strong bunch of young men and high expectations. Wyoming at this time in history was a small but affluent town that reflected all the good things about those types of communities. People knew everyone, everyone knew them and all of them felt safe. It was a prosperous, happy place that seemed somewhat unaffected by the major ebbs and flows that history tells us shaped kids at the time. The cheerleaders were the prettiest and smartest girls in the school, and there was a pep rally every Friday before the games. The football team wore coats and ties to school the day of the game. All of them played other sports, and almost all of them played both ways in football. Their dates would wait outside the locker room for the guys to shower and dress and go with them to get a burger at the Frisch's Big Boy or maybe the Corral.

His squad had some big linemen that year, and his philosophy was to keep the offense simple, liking to run a lot of quick hitters to get his backs into the opponent's backfield quickly and accelerate them past any potential tacklers. One special lineman was Mandell Gentry, a 260-pounder who was rarely, if ever, moved off the line by anyone.

The coach ran an offensive scheme called a "Belly Series" from a T-formation that emphasized optioning the ball to anyone in the backfield. Wayne "Bing"

Guckenberger was the Cowboys' senior quarterback, and it was noted that they did not throw much, especially with him in there, as they only threw three touchdown passes all year, one to his backup at QB, Bobby Goodrich, whom Bing modestly noted was a better thrower than he was, although Coach Lewis thought highly enough of Bing to let him audible when and where necessary. On defense, in true teenage competitive fashion, Bing and Bobby had personal competitions to see who would get the most tackles.

Lewis ran tightly disciplined, timed practice sessions and had his charges drill and drill on the fundamentals of blocking and tackling. He was very much a motivator but was not abusive in any way. During practices and games, he did not tolerate trash talking or fighting, and woe be on your head if you did either, for you would have to work your way back into the starting lineup as punishment if a player committed either infraction. His was a total team concept. The skilled positions were smaller than most of their opponents but were highly skilled athletes who could play with anyone. Because of this disparity in size, everyone doing their job, with no prima donnas was the rule. While his numbers to draw on were small, Coach Lewis still valued competition for each job and had a Tackling Trophy that he awarded each week to the hardest tackler. When you did something well or even spectacularly, he might give you a nod of the head or a pat on the butt, but not much more. Again, it was all about the team and not the individual.

He valued scouting reports and in games seemed to magically know what defense to call against a play or player. In fact, he thought you could score more on defense than you could on offense. He showed that thinking on special teams also, setting up schemes resulting in the Cowboys returning fifteen punts for touchdowns in 1961 and 1962. During the 1962 season, all this coaching and drilling and player's skill would come into play to deliver to the world a season that is so rare nowadays that it is almost unbelievable to imagine.

Norwood High School was the first scheduled regular season game for the Cowboys. As far back as 1809, travelers were staying at a coach stop at the intersection of Smith and Montgomery Roads. The surrounding area harbored about fifty people, and over time it became known as Sharpsburg and then later Norwood. Schools were built as early as 1838, and Norwood High dates to the late 1890s. It had played football for many years as the Indians. Separated by only 8.4 miles and called the Cowboys and Indians, these Norwood and Wyoming teams formed a natural matchup.

It was Wyoming that won this year's edition of a decades-old, traditional battle, 40–0. Woodward Heights was next and was Wyoming's version of

Massillon Washington and Canton McKinley. It was a tough one, but the Cowboys walked off the field with an 18–0 victory.

The wins just kept on coming:

- Mariemont, 28–0
- De Porres, 51–0
- Mount Healthy, 35–0
- Greenhills, 44–0
- Ready, 34–0
- Deer Park, 78–0
- Lockland, 68–0
- N.C.H., 46–0

Bing Guckenberger said that the team soon realized what was happening, that they might be doing something spectacular that had been done once before by the Wyoming Cowboys in 1942: go undefeated, untied and unscored on. They did and wrote themselves into history—for the second time! Unscored on 446–0!

The Wyoming High School football program of the 1960s was nothing short of spectacular. After the 1962 season, the Cowboys went 10-0 for the next two seasons—who does that remind you of? Massillon Washington, maybe, or how about Fostoria? Upper Arlington, Cleveland St. Ignatius and Cincinnati Moeller come to mind in later years. Yes, in the 1960s, Wyoming could be compared to these schools and more. After three straight 10-0 seasons, the Cowboys of Bob Lewis put 8-1 and 9-1 records on their résumé and then slipped to 6-3-1 in 1967 before returning to complete dominance with 9-0 and 10-0 records to close out the decade at 88-6-4, for a winning percentage of 87 percent! During this time, their losses were to much bigger schools like Colerain, Anderson, Woodward and Princeton—all giants out of the growing football factories of Cincinnati.

But of all those years, it is 1962 people still talk about, the sixty-five kids who supported their small team, coached by one of the legends of Ohio coaching, cheering them to an unforgettable season.

Coach Bob Lewis died on September 24, 2009, at age eighty-three; he was living in Somerset, Kentucky, at the time of his death. Wyoming's stadium is named after Lewis, who had a 198-21-7 record in twenty-three years at Wyoming. He had eleven undefeated seasons during his tenure and not one losing season. Wyoming was Class AA state runner-up in 1975 and state champion in '77. Lewis then moved to Kentucky and coached Conner High School to the 1980

Kentucky Class AAA state finals, losing there to Franklin-Simpson. Three years later, he was there again and won the school's only football state championship for them, beating Franklin-Simpson, 12–7, for the Class AAA title.

Coach Lewis had a lifetime coaching record of 270-55-8 and is in the Wyoming High School and the Ohio High School Football Coaches Hall of Fame.

1962 Black Hole: Canton McKinley High School

Sometime in the 1960–61 period, there appeared a ripple in the Canton, Ohio continuum when two Canton McKinley fans, boosters, tourists or whatever they were called back then were visiting Portsmouth, Ohio, and started something with disastrous results. Hearing that a few Portsmouth football playing brothers were not getting satisfying playing time, they helped the father of these two boys get a job in the Canton area, and they then joined Canton McKinley's football team for the 1961 season. Bad move by all concerned. Queue the music!

The superintendent of the Portsmouth School System reported this "abduction" of "two of his star players" to the Ohio High School Athletic Association (OHSAA), or, in this telling, that unnamed government agency, and a movie of the week ensued. McKinley had evidently violated a bylaw called "undue influence" and was banned from playing football in 1962.

The problem with this script was that the players in question reportedly weren't that good anyway. The father of the two boys was supposedly upset that his sons didn't play more, but hey, in Canton you earn it, right? McKinley took this thing all the way to the state Supreme Court and lost. The cool thing about the "death penalty" that OHSAA imposed was that McKinley created an intramural program with multiple teams, and the Massillon band stopped by one time to play for its rival. Hatred does take holidays. Thirteen players got financial aid to college to play football because of this program. I liked that part of the script.

Because of the negative public relations that ensued from its decision, OHSAA never again imposed such a penalty. Smart move. Like any school, including colleges, it cannot control boosters and what they do. The two McKinley fans had done nothing different than many had done and what private schools had done for decades: recruit players.

As Michael T. George said on the Canton McKinley Bulldogs website, the 1962 Bulldogs were "Undefeated, Untied, and Undressed."

1963

Powerful Niles McKinley returned to the title spot in 1963, followed by Massillon Washington and the Sandusky Blue Streaks at nos. 2 and 3, respectively. Toledo Central Catholic had the football gods shine a very bright light on it in '62 but would not appear in the Top 10 for the rest of the decade.

The Red Dragons were on a thirty-seven-game winning streak entering 1963 with a great coaching staff instructing them and both sides of the ball practicing against some of the best players in the Midwest. Niles McKinley became nationally known, and sport writers from around the nation clamored for more background so they could write their stories about the team.

Their season was epic in its drama and reminds one of a movie script. The Red Dragons went undefeated, tying once, and winning the needed votes to claim another championship. In doing so, they extended their unbeaten streak to forty-seven. They delivered seven shutouts, with one team scoring on a punt return. They whipped Toledo Scott 60–22 (the Niles first and second teams were already showered and dressed, watching the rest of the game in street clothes) and Farrell 27–6 to round out the season. Although undefeated, it wasn't a perfect run.

The Cincinnati Roger Bacon Spartans, extremely powerful and a team many claimed had the best talent in the state—better than the Red Dragons even—lined up against Niles in the fourth game of the year. They were both 3-0 at the time, and for the first and only time during Niles's unbeaten streak, an opponent beat it in the statistics. As if Hollywood wrote it, the Spartans had the ball at the Niles 6-yard line with just a few seconds left and missed a field goal; 0–0 was the score touted in the headline the next day.

A few days after its final win of the season, Niles was voted state champs by both the AP and UPI voters. Waiting at Alberini's Restaurant, an estimated three hundred players, coaches and fans got the word and paraded through town in celebration.

Niles opened the 1964 season with a 54–0 win over Cleveland East Tech under new head coach Glen Stennett. The following week, more than thirty thousand fans jammed the Akron Rubber Bowl to witness Niles's forty-eight-game winning streak end in a 14–8 loss to Massillon.

Niles McKinley's run through the early '60s was amazing and stands as one of the highlights of Ohio high school football. The talent the team had along with outstanding coaches and strong community support made it the

Top: The 1963 Sandusky High School football team. That year was Earle Bruce's last as Blue Streaks coach, and his staff included four assistants who would also go on to become head coaches: Bob Seaman succeeded him as coach at Sandusky and Massillon, John Behling would spend a year as Fremont Ross's coach before returning to New Philadelphia and serving as coach there, Gene Kidwell would serve as Sandusky head coach and Tony Munafo would serve as coach in nearby Huron. *Courtesy Gene Kidwell.*

Bottom: The '63 Niles McKinley team enters the field in their traditional way, led by Captain Frank Lutz. *Courtesy www.nilesdragons.com.*

perfect candidate to dethrone Massillon and the other powers and become the giant-killer of legend.

Sandusky, in Earle Bruce's last year, went 9-0-1 and finished behind a one-loss Massillon team.

1963 OHIO AP STATE POLL
1. Niles (9-0-1)
2. Massillon (9-1)—lost to Akron Garfield
3. Sandusky (9-0-1)
4. Cincinnati Roger Bacon (9-0-1)
5. Cleveland St. Ignatius (9-0)
6. Akron Garfield (9-0-1)—defeated Massillon
7. Springfield South (9-1)
8. Dayton Roth (9-0)
9. Fremont St. Joseph (9-0)
10. Ashland (10-0)

1964

The year 1964 was one to reflect more prominently on the turmoil of the world situation and the dissatisfaction of people, although in Massillon, when the state championship returned to the confines of that magical enclave in Stark County, all was normal again. Coach Earle Bruce had moved from Sandusky to Massillon to coach the Tigers, and the effect was dramatic. The Tigers finished no. 1 in Ohio and no. 2 in the nation this year.

Sandusky finished 7th in the Ohio AP Poll. A team from outside Columbus, Upper Arlington, finished up ahead of the Blue Streaks in 6th, and people started to watch them closely. Springfield South at no. 3 was the only other team not from the northern half of the state in the Top 10.

As noted in the 1963 section on Niles, Massillon broke the Red Dragon's forty-eight-game unbeaten streak with a 14–8 victory at the Akron Rubber Bowl in front of 30,128 fans at the beginning of the '64 season. But there was another McKinley in Stark County that also wanted a say about the Tigers' destiny. Massillon and Canton McKinley were both 9-0 entering the finale in 1964 and ranked no. 1 and no. 2, respectively, in the AP Poll. The game was broadcast on Cleveland television. The Bulldogs jumped to a

Right: Canton McKinley versus Massillon, November 14, 1964. *Courtesy Canton City Schools.*

Below: The 1964 Sandusky High School football team. *Courtesy Gene Kidwell.*

14–0 lead at the half, but the Tigers came back to score 20 in the last quarter to win the game and be voted to another state championship.

Massillon's coach, Earle Bruce, successful everywhere he coached, would ultimately go on to Ohio State and win a lot of games. Don Nehlen, Canton McKinley's coach, would go on to coach West Virginia and enjoy an equally successful career there.

St. Ignatius High School Wildcats

Cleveland-based St. Ignatius High School was officially founded on September 6, 1886. At that time, St. Ignatius was the twentieth secondary school sponsored by the Jesuits in the United States. A superb college preparatory school that has taken eager kids into areas of higher learning encompassing just about every field imaginable, its football program has been near the top many times, and in the early 1960s, Coach John Wirtz and his staff put together one of the greatest teams in the history of Ohio high school football, the 10-0 City Champion led by one of the best do-it-all athletes ever to come out of Ohio: senior quarterback/safety Brian Dowling.

St. Ignatius wrapped up the 1964 season with a 48–6 victory over Benedictine in the annual Thanksgiving Day Charity Game in front of 41,183 fans. They got a show, as on the second play from scrimmage Dowling took it himself 71 yards for a touchdown. Of course, he also played defense. He was so good, in fact, he ended his high school football career with thirty-three interceptions, the Ohio state record for career interceptions that still stands today.

Dowling, with offers from sixty schools, including Ohio State and Notre Dame, went to Yale to play football, rooming with teammate Calvin Hill, and both guys would enjoy stellar collegiate and pro careers. Both players would play in "The Game," the famous 1968 Yale-Harvard contest of undefeated teams that ended in a 29–29 and which Harvard claimed it had won because in the last forty-two seconds, it scored 16 points to tie it. Playing on the Crimson team was Tommy Lee Jones (All-Ivy at tackle), the future actor. A 2008 documentary directed by Kevin Rafferty was filmed about this game, *Harvard Beats Yale 29–29*, and it got great reviews.

Brian's athletic careers at St. Ignatius and Yale at that point were so renowned that he became the model for a regular character, "B.D.," in the *Bull Tales* comic strip written for the *Yale Daily News* by a Yale classmate named Garry Trudeau. A few years later, it morphed into *Doonesbury*, becoming the first daily comic strip to win a Pulitzer Prize.

The Barberton Magics: A Sad Story about the Fragility of Life

Going into their 1964 game with the Alliance Aviators, the Magics were undefeated and going for their thirteenth straight win spanning two seasons. Quarterbacking the Magics was six-foot-one, 185-pound All-District Ken Sennett, a kid who was being recruited by Ohio State and other big-time programs. On Thursday morning, the day before the Alliance game, Ken put his head down on his desk in English class and never woke up. He died two hours later at the hospital. No injury had been previously reported. The entire community was staggered. Later, it was determined that Ken had a rare heart defect. Still dazed, the team wanted to go ahead and play Alliance to honor Ken but just could not summon enough for a win, losing 14–8 and ending their winning streak. It had been Homecoming, and the Saturday night party was called off. Ken had been one of the candidates for Homecoming King. Ken Sennett was survived by his mom and dad; two sisters, Cynthia, fifteen, and Patricia, thirteen; and two brothers, James, eleven, and John, six months old.

1964 OHIO AP STATE POLL

1. Massillon (10-0) (also 2nd in national poll)—defeated Canton McKinley, Niles
2. Canton McKinley (9-1)—lost to Massillon
3. Springfield South (10-0)
4. Elyria (9-1)
5. Louisville (10-0)
6. Upper Arlington (9-0)
7. Sandusky (9-1)
8. Rossford (9-0)
9. Cleveland St. Ignatius (9-0)
10. Fremont St. Joseph (9-0)

1965

The Tigers of Coach Earle Bruce repeated in 1965, again going 10-0, winning the Associated Press state voting and finishing 2nd on the national scene, with Sandusky finishing at 10-0 and in 2nd place in the AP. Both years, though, the Tigers had some close calls. In 1964, they got by Niles McKinley by just 14–8, while the Bulldogs of Canton McKinley lost by just 6, 20–14. In 1965, it was even tighter: Massillon edged Warren Harding, 16–12, and then just eked out a victory over the Bulldogs in the last game of the season, 18–14. The year 1965 also started Massillon on a thirty-two-game unbeaten streak that would end in 1966.

The story of Ohio high school football in 1965 was not so much Massillon going undefeated and winning another AP Poll championship. That wasn't news, although it was getting a little boring. It was Sandusky winning the UPI state championship and Massillon coming in after it.

The Blue Streaks of Sandusky High School were an extremely powerful football team in 1965, probably one of the finest in the school's history. The "Monsters of the Seaway" became one of only six Sandusky High School teams to go undefeated and were the first in thirty years. They scored an average of 36.6 points and held the opposition to a mere 3.4 points per game average. Going into the 1965 season, they were led by tri-captains Brian Healy (QB), Dave Schweinfurth (tackle) and Dan Kaser (end).

These guys took the rest of the team into the first game against Lakewood and started slowly, but after an interception by Bill Deming, they went 77

Canton McKinley battles Massillon Washington on November 13, 1965. *Courtesy www. cantonrep.com.*

Left: Sandusky High School alumnus Cleveland Dickerson would go on to play college football at Miami University. *Courtesy Miami University Athletics.*

Below: Canton McKinley versus Massillon, November 13, 1965. *Courtesy Canton City Schools.*

yards for the TD, their great running back Cleveland Dickerson going over from the 1-yard line. Brian Healy later added a TD to end it 16–0. They whipped John Marshall out of Cleveland, 42–0, for their second victory and then met up with Toledo Woodward. Brian Healy threw for two touchdowns and David LeVier scored two more as the Blue Streaks won, 31–6.

In their Buckeye Conference opener against the Marion Harding Presidents, Sandusky annihilated the Prexies, 51–14, scoring the first seven times the team had the ball and leading Harding 51–0 with eight minutes to play in the third quarter. Fullback Cleveland Dickerson and Brian Healy each scored twice, and in the first quarter, Healy threw a 52-yard touchdown pass to George Garrett. It was total domination from beginning to end over the suffering Marion Harding team.

The Blue Streaks beat Lorain Senior, 44–0, in the fifth game of the season and then traveled to Findlay, where they won easily, 30–6, with Brian Healy completing ten out of ten passing. Bill Deming got his third and fourth interceptions of the season. An always tough Elyria squad was next, and Coach Seaman's guys took advantage of a blocked punt and a fumble to make their first two scores and beat the Pioneers, 26–0, their fourth shutout in seven games.

Brian Healy had a great day in the Streaks' next game against Fremont Ross, completing five of six attempts for 205 yards and three touchdowns, all to George Garrett. Junior halfback Arry Keys got 138 yards on seven carries and scored twice. Sandusky totaled 552 yards of total offense and came away with a 54–0 shellacking of their longtime rival.

Against Lorain Admiral King the next week, they clinched their fifth Buckeye Conference Championship in the past six years by winning 24–8. The final game of the year was against Mansfield Senior, and the Blue Streaks rolled up 521 yards and won handily, 48–0, against the mewing Tygers.

The UPI voted Sandusky the no. 1 high school football team in Ohio in 1965, state champs, sharing the honor with Massillon, which had won the Associated Press mythical title. The UPI's balloting was the closest it had been since it began voting on high school teams twelve years earlier. Sandusky got eighteen 1st-place votes and 379 points, while Massillon Washington got sixteen 1st-place votes and 375 points. In the final five weeks of the season, Sandusky had gained 105 points on Washington and clinched the state title. The final UPI Poll looked like this in 1965:

School	1st Place	Pts.
Sandusky	18	379
Massillon Washington	16	375
Warren Harding		197
Cincinnati Moeller	4	172
Upper Arlington	1	153
Middletown		142
Columbus Bishop Watterson	2	138
Lima Senior	1	119
Steubenville		98
Cleveland Benedictine		94

In the Associated Press, Massillon Washington was voted into 1st place by 18 points, 162 to Sandusky's 144.

At the Blue Streaks' banquet following the season, Woody Hayes spoke and multiple players were recognized for their accomplishments. Eleven Sandusky players made All–Buckeye Conference. The team MVP honor was shared by Brian Healy and Schweinfurth, while center Werner Hall was Sandusky's Lineman of the Year. The Associated Press elected Dave Schweinfurth and Dave LeVier to its All-Ohio team, while Healy got the honor as well. Coach Seaman was UPI Coach of the Year.

Coach Seaman described the just completed championship season as "great and marvelous." Regarding his young charges, he said, "I am glad to be associated with such a great group of boys. I was glad to see football played the way it should be, with hitting, desire, and determination. Every member of the squad was dedicated to winning, and each one made sacrifices to ensure our ten victories."

1966

Massillon and Canton McKinley both suffered this year. Massillon ended up 4-5-1, and Canton McKinley ended up 6-4. Still, their season-ending battle was attended by 19,009 fans, with the Bulldogs winning, 25–16.

Sandusky High School's 1965 football season had been a banner year, and like all banner years, the expectations following are sometimes set for the same results. That's not a bad thing; it's just that sometimes a letdown is the order of the day and not a repeat or betterment of the previous year. In this case, Coach Seaman left Sandusky to travel east to Massillon, where he assumed the head coaching job there from Earle Bruce, who had gone to Ohio State University. Replacing him was Bob Reublin, and while the new coach had lost some quality players from the '65 squad, he had twelve lettermen and others were stepping up in practice and would see a lot of playing time in 1966. Willie Amison, Bill Deming and Vic Malinovsky would be tri-captains for 1966.

In its 1966 opener with Lakewood, which it won, 16–6, Arry Keys had a 94-yard kickoff return. The next game was with Cleveland East, and the Blue Streaks easily handled the team, 38–8, with Willie Amison scoring on a 51-yard pass reception from QB Bill Deming. Ed Williams, an emerging runner of spectacular power and ability, ran for 212 yards in seventeen carries against Toledo Woodward in leading them to a 46–0 victory. Williams

This page: Massillon versus Canton McKinley, November 12, 1966. *Courtesy Canton City Schools.*

would go on to gain 3,155 yards during three years with the Blue Streaks and play for West Virginia. There, he would gain 208 yards and earn Most Valuable Offensive Player at the Peach Bowl while breaking WVU's single-game rushing mark.

As Sandusky headed into its Buckeye Conference opener with Marion Harding, it was ranked no. 1 in the UPI. The Blue Streaks once again

The 1966 Sandusky High School football team. *Courtesy Gene Kidwell.*

manhandled Harding, scoring the first four times they had the ball in a fourteen-minute span. Bill Deming had a 68-yard punt return and an interception, with the Blue Streaks scoring after each turnover. Sandusky ran into a tougher foe the following game, when it just got by always gnarly Lima Senior by just 20–12.

Findlay was defeated the next game, 36–6, and then the Blue Streaks focused their attention on the undefeated Elyria team who were coming up that week. In beating the Pioneers, 20–12, defensive tackle Willie Shaw was cited for his efforts in stopping the strong offense of this northern Ohio powerhouse.

An amazing effort was next on the program, as the Blue Streaks caught Fremont Ross in a down year and mishandled the team to the tune of 74–0, with Sandusky scoring eleven touchdowns and gaining 677 total yards in a very embarrassing loss for the Little Giants. Deming tossed three TDs to George Garrett, and Ed Williams and Willie Amison each scored two. The Buckeye Conference title was secured the following game when Sandusky beat Lorain Admiral King, 46–6, with Amison going 73 yards on the first play from scrimmage for a TD. Keys, Williams and Tom Darden each scored twice. The last game of the season was a 34–0 victory over Mansfield Senior.

The year 1966 was a thrilling one in Ohio high school football, with several teams battling throughout the season for the top spot. It wasn't until the last week of the season that the title was decided, and it turned out to be Columbus Bishop Watterson, whose fantastic run to the crown will be detailed soon and whose team were a unanimous choice for no. 1. Niles McKinley finished second and Sandusky third in both polls. The UPI Poll

The cover of the 1966 Ross-Sandusky game program. *Courtesy Vince Guerrieri.*

was very close (394 to 392 to 382 points, respectively), while the AP showed equally narrow margins (206 to 201 to 190 points, respectively).

Vic Malinovsky was selected by the Blue Streaks as their MVP and Lineman of the Year. He also was an All–Buckeye Conference pick on both sides of the ball and was Lineman of the Year in Ohio in the UPI and first-team All-Ohio on the Associated Press team. George Garrett made All-Ohio honors as well. Malinovsky made high school All-American and won the Malinovsky Award, named after his father and given to a senior male for excellence in the classroom and in athletics.

During the 1960s, Sandusky High School was one of the best big-school teams the state could offer. Its record for this decade is seen here:

1960	9-1
1961	8-2
1962	8-0-2
1963	9-0-1
1964	9-1
1965	10-0
1966	10-0
1967	9-1
1968	7-3
1969	8-2

This record of 87-10-3 tallies up to a winning percentage of 88.32 over ten years, an outstanding accomplishment and one that the student body and the community were justifiably proud of and savor to this day.

The other story in Sandusky in 1966 was that of Sandusky St. Mary, which finished 10-0 as well. It was a great time in Sandusky these years if you were a high school football fan.

Then Again, So Was Bishop Watterson's Record

Bishop Watterson High School, founded in 1954 in Columbus, Ohio, is a very rigorous academic prep school with an almost 100 percent graduation and high college attendance rates that has traditionally fielded some of the toughest football teams in central Ohio. Named in honor of Bishop John Ambrose Watterson, the Second Bishop of Columbus, in 1966 the Eagles played in the Catholic Central League and used Westerville North's field as their home field because they had no space for one of their own. This same model was used in Marion with Marion Catholic sharing Marion Harding's field, with the Irish playing on Saturday nights when both had home games. Entering this year, the Eagles had a nine-game winning streak going, having been unbeaten in 1965 and finishing 4th in the final Associated Press Poll, following Massillon Washington, Sandusky and Cincinnati Moeller, while being followed in 5th by Warren Harding and then Columbus-area rival Upper Arlington at 6th. Cleveland Benedictine, Steubenville High School, Athens and Middletown rounded out the final Top 10 that year.

Bishop Watterson played in the Central Catholic League, and South was in the City League. The Catholic schools were matched up that night against several City Leaguers, coming out on top in three contests. In two of them, Bishop Ready shut out Whetstone, 18–0, and Columbus DeSales just barely got past Linden McKinley, 14–12. In the third, Watterson took apart South, 38–0. The game was decided quickly in the first quarter when the Eagles scored two TDs and extra points, gaining 219 of their final 470 yards. Five different Eagles crossed the goal line, with quarterback John Motil's 35-yarder the longest. It was a strong opening performance, and Watterson seemed like it hadn't lost a step from its 1965 winning ways.

North High School was next, and Watterson's confident strides continued, the Eagles again dominating and walking off the field with a 44–0 smasher.

After two games, Bishop Watterson led the area teams in several vital statistics, scoring 82 points against 0 for their opponents. Upper Arlington was second with 77 points scored versus 30 scored against it.

In a non-league game for their third outing of the year, the Eagles traveled to Lancaster, Ohio, to play the Golden Gales of Lancaster High School. The outcome of this game was a little closer than the previous two games, but not by much. The Lancaster team, quarterbacked by a kid named Rex Kern (future Ohio State QB and Baltimore Colt), led at halftime, 14–12. But the second half was a different story, with Coach Dick Walker getting the Eagles to play up to their abilities. Watterson scored 20 points to Lancaster's 6 and came home with a 38–20 win.

The UPI Poll published the following week showed Sandusky in 1st place, tied with Warren Harding at 190 points each. Massillon Washington, Steubenville and Niles followed them, with Upper Arlington at 6th, Mansfield Senior at 7th and Watterson coming in at 8th place. Cincinnati Roger Bacon and Cleveland St. Joseph rounded out the rest of the Top 10. The Eagles still led in central Ohio stats with 120 points scored and 20 against. The next opponent on the schedule was Columbus West High School.

In what seemed to be a replay of how Watterson was winning, fullback Joe Schultheis scored three times, one on a 48-yard runner, racking up 142 yards on sixteen rumbles. The defense of Coach Walker was magnificent, holding West from penetrating past the Eagles' 40, and the offense scored within the first two minutes, going 57 yards for the easy TD, thanks to Schultheis's 33-yard gallop and then 1-yard plunge for the score. It was a 28–0 victory for the Eagles.

After this game, the UPI voted the Eagles at 6th place, right behind Upper Arlington at 5th, in its October 4 poll. In the Associated Press Poll the same week, Upper Arlington was 5th, but Watterson was 9th. Sandusky was still at the top in the UPI but alone this week since Warren Harding had lost to the Big Red of Steubenville, 21–8. Steubenville was no. 2 but was no. 1 in the AP Poll. Lima Senior was in 8th place in the AP but was no. 11 in the UPI.

In the October 5 *Columbus Dispatch* edition, the headline was, "Arlington, Watterson Keep Collision Course," and when someone around town mentioned "the game," it was with a knowing nod that they were talking about the November 11 date when the two powerhouses would meet. But first Arlington had to beat the 3-0-1 Massillon Washington Tigers on October 21. The Eagles were due to travel to Newark for their next battle, with the Wildcats hoping to rebound from a loss to Upper Arlington the previous week in a driving rainstorm. The Golden Bears were playing Mount Vernon that week.

It was a night that benefited the Eagles. They defeated Newark, 30–7, but trailed for the first time that season, falling behind, 8–7, at the half but rebounding easily. Upper Arlington, meanwhile, demolished Mount Vernon, 60–6. But the two games that benefited the Eagles the most were Mansfield Senior losing, 20–14, to Lorain Admiral King and Lima Senior losing to Hamilton Garfield, 41–0. Senior and Mansfield had both been ahead of the Eagles in the AP Poll going into that weekend.

In the new polls, Watterson was still 6th in the UPI and 8th in the AP, while the Golden Bears were 4th in both. Niles McKinley beat Massillon Washington, 20–12, stopping the Tigers' thirty-three-game unbeaten streak. Niles was 3rd in both polls. Steubenville and Sandusky were no. 1 in both. Marion Catholic at 5-0 was no. 1 in the Class A division. Because of their huge point total, the Golden Bears of Upper Arlington were now leading the greater Franklin County teams in statistics, with 187 points scored against 48 given up, with Watterson right behind them.

In the October 13 *Columbus Dispatch*, it was noted that Upper Arlington had charted twenty-five buses for the trip to Massillon a week from Friday night, the first time ever the two teams had met, and that three thousand tickets had been allocated to the Bears. However, even with this big game on the docket, it was also noted that advance ticket sales for the Watterson–Upper Arlington games would go on sale the following week. That game, to be held at UA's home field, would only hold 4,200, and the *Columbus Dispatch* writer Lou Berliner said that if the game were held in a larger venue, it would draw 20,000 or more. The Golden Bears were slated to host DeSales that week, and the Eagles were hosting Bishop Ready at the North High field on Saturday.

The Friday night game against DeSales almost proved Upper Arlington's undoing, with the Golden Bears getting into a whale of a fight with the DeSales boys and Arlington barely winning its Homecoming game, 29–20. It was an even game, and with five minutes remaining, the Bears' Brian Kitchen tossed a 34-yard TD pass to John Fickell—the Upper Arlington staff started to feel somewhat secure but not wholly. The Eagles of Bishop Watterson won their game easily.

Next week, Bob Seaman, the coach of Massillon Washington High School (he had come to Massillon from Sandusky High School), said after the Golden Bears whipped his team, 21–6, that the "Bears were as good as or better than any team they had faced that season." It was a huge win for Upper Arlington and central Ohio in general, and Coach Marv Morehead said of his team that it was one of the top performances he had ever seen. The win set the stage still more for their upcoming tilt with Bishop Watterson.

Watterson, having beaten Dayton Alter the same weekend in a close one, fell from 5th to 6th in the AP but remained 5th in the UPI. The Top 5 teams in both polls were undefeated—a nice change from the usual. Coming up for the Eagles was a battle with Columbus DeSales.

Upper Arlington beat an energized Worthington team, 19–7, on the following Friday night, and on that Saturday evening, Bishop Watterson ripped DeSales, 52–0, at a game played at Brookhaven's field. Several different Eagles scored for Watterson, and the score at halftime was 30–0. Watterson for the game had eighteen first downs and 362 yards rushing and hit on five of fifteen passes for 115 yards, while the defense intercepted five passes! It was truly a dominating performance and equal to, if not better than, any performance that any team in the state had put up that season. The tension in the Columbus area grew, and conversations around the state were becoming focused on that November 11 game.

When the polls were released on November 1, the Columbus community had three teams in the Top 10 in the AP, with Upper Arlington 2nd in the AP and 3rd in the UPI; Bishop Watterson was 6th in the AP and 5th in the UPI. Columbus Eastmoor was ranked 10th in the AP and 12th in the UPI. This was a first that season and made the central Ohio area very proud. Steubenville was first on both polls.

Coach Bob Stuart's Eastmoor 8-0 squad entered City League competition in 1958 and had won a few titles in their brief history, but this season was one of the best since the '61 team went 10-0. Watterson was traveling to play Hartley at 7:30 p.m. Saturday—Upper Arlington was playing at Cambridge the night before. It was pretty football crazy that early November in central Ohio.

Well, high school football is constantly full of surprises, and the old saying of "that's why they play the games" was in full definition that weekend. In a huge upset in front of 17,404 screaming people, Massillon Washington shut out Steubenville's no. 1 Big Red, 12–0; this stunner paved the way for the Golden Bears of Upper Arlington to ascend to the no. 1 spot come next week. It appeared that there would be a mad scramble in the Top 10, and the other games that weekend showed that no one was backing down. Upper Arlington devastated Cambridge, 40–0; Sandusky beat Lorain Admiral King, 44–6; 5th-ranked Hamilton Garfield whipped Hamilton Taft, 27–8; and Watterson crashed the goal line for a pair of fourth-quarter touchdowns to beat Hartley, 24–6, and win the Central Catholic League Championship.

It was the ninth win that year for Coach Dick Walker, his Eagles unbeaten and untied (eighteen straight), and the school and community were getting amped up for their next game: the Golden Bears from across town. The last time Watterson had lost a game was to Newark High School, by one point, on October 9, 1964. In this next-to-last game of 1966, Joe Schultheis scored three touchdowns for the Eagles and snagged four points on two conversion attempts.

Hyperbole, from the ancient Greek, is something one does to exaggerate, evoke strong feelings or create a strong impression. In the case of Bishop Watterson traveling the streets and byways of Columbus to get to the Upper Arlington stadium, hyperbole took the form of describing this game as the "Game of the Century." Both teams carried long unbeaten streaks: the Golden Bears at twenty-eight and the Eagles at twenty-two. The game was sold out in advance and was to be televised locally.

The Tuesday AP Poll of November 8 had the Golden Bears in the No. 1 slot, a first for a Columbus-area team in the almost twenty-year history of the polls. The UPI had Sandusky up top with UA after it. Watterson was voted 5th in the AP and 4th in the UPI, respectively. Columbus Eastmoor was 8th in the AP and 12th in the UPI.

As with any big game, analysis was the order of the day, and the *Columbus Dispatch* presented one with comments from several coaches around the area and the state. Forrest Sharrock, coach of DeSales, stated flatly that "Arlington's band will outshine Watterson's." Watterson did not field a band! But in all seriousness, the consensus was that it was an even bet. Brian Kitchen of Upper Arlington and John Motil of Watterson were the quarterbacks, and both were very good. Kitchen was six feet and 168 pounds, and Motil was the same height but 12 pounds heavier. Both were projected as college quarterbacks and both labeled as runners first and passers second in the offenses they led, but both could pass well when called on.

Upper Arlington had not lost a game since a 12-11 loss to Mount Vernon on October 25, 1963. It was noted around the state that the power shift from northeast Ohio was moving to the central section of the state. Certainly, a case could be made for such a claim. Coach Moorehead of UA dispelled such pretensions, saying he thought "the northeast emphasized football more than other locales and perhaps they are a bit more vociferous than schools in the south." He also said that they wanted a victory over Watterson in the worst way. Asked about a tie, he said, "A tie never entered my mind. That would be like kissing your sister." A tie would just be unthinkable!

On the front page of the *Columbus Dispatch* the day after the game was a little block that read, "U. ARLINGTON TROUNCED 32–0 BY WATTERSON." Yes, that's right: 32–0!

Coach Dick Walker said after the game, "This has to be the greatest team I've ever coached." Coach Moorehead of Upper Arlington lamented, "9-1 is not a bad record—when you lose to the best team in Ohio."

Walker's record at Watterson was 51-11-3, while Moorehead's was 85-23-3—records any coach, regardless of the region of the state they were from, would be envious of. Earlier that week, Coach Walker had said that his senior halfback, Tim Wagner, was the most underrated and overlooked running back in central Ohio. Wagner must have heard his coach's comments, as he racked up 261 yards rushing in sixteen tries and one pass reception for 16 yards, scoring two TDs in the process. Moorehead conceded that just about everything Watterson did that night was perfect.

About 7,500 standing room–only fans attended this televised gigantic game, the largest Upper Arlington home crowd since 1949; 36 policemen controlled the throng. While this doesn't compare statistically to Massillon or Cleveland crowds, it was nonetheless just as intense. It was the first shutout of an Upper Arlington football team since Whitehall beat them,

21–0, in a Central Buckeye League game played on October 13, 1963. Coach Walker said, "This was the greatest game any Watterson team ever played. We knew we had to contain Brian Kitchen, so we changed our whole defensive set-up and used the Eagles on their strong side and showed the Oklahoma on the weak side, rotating with him and going hard if he started up the field."

Moorehead thought that they could win at halftime, even though they trailed 20–0. He said, "Watterson was a great team tonight," and admitted that the Eagles surprised them. It is always tough to comment after a loss and especially so when the loser had not tasted defeat for so long and then to lose on your home field. It was evident that his comments were safe and guarded in reflecting on what had just happened.

The Eagles' defensive studs of Jim Woltz, Mike Mahley, John Strange and Mike Hilliard limited the Bears to just 37 yards rushing! It was a great effort on Watterson's part to play tough football against a tough football team, and the effect of such an effort evidently caught the Golden Bears off their game.

Who would be no. 1? That was the question posed in the *Columbus Dispatch* on Sunday, November 13. Niles McKinley had beaten Warren Harding, 22–6, and the Blue Streaks whipped Mansfield Senior, 34–0. Who would look the best to the pollsters? They, along with Watterson, were 10-0. But Hamilton Garfield finished 9-0, as did Columbus Eastmoor. Louisville had finished 10-0 and had gotten its thirty-eighth win over four seasons, beating Minerva, 20–0. Who would it be?

Thousands saw the Watterson–Upper Arlington game on television and would never forget it. Watterson's claim to the state title was a strong one: it had beaten the no. 1 in the state—what more needed to be done? The polls released on November 15–16 would give everyone an answer.

"Eagles Take It All" was the headline on the sports page of the *Columbus Dispatch*, dated November 16, 1966. The AP Poll had Bishop Watterson no. 1 over Niles by five votes, 206 to 201. Sandusky was next, followed by Steubenville, Hamilton Garfield, Upper Arlington, Columbus Eastmoor, Akron Hoban, Louisville and Liverpool. This was a jump from no. 5 to no. 1 in one week. In the UPI Poll released the day before, the Eagles were in the top spot by an equally close margin of only 2 points, 394 to 392, as voted by the fifty-one coaches who voted. This margin was the closest in the history of the UPI ratings.

It was an outstanding showing by the Bishop Watterson team of Coach Dick Walker, the first time ever a team from outside the northern sector had made no. 1 since the AP began voting. In the UPI voting, Arlington came in at 5th place, followed by Hamilton Garfield, Akron Hoban, Cincinnati Elder, Lima Senior and Mentor. A side-by-side comparison shows the differences in the way the two AA polls thought in 1966:

UPI	Points	AP	Points
Watterson	394	Watterson	206
Niles	392	Niles	201
Sandusky	382	Sandusky	190
Steubenville	232	Steubenville	120
Upper Arlington	164	Hamilton Garfield	101
Hamilton Garfield	158	Upper Arlington	99
Akron Hoban	158	Columbus Eastmoor	64
Cincinnati Elder	76	Akron Hoban	55
Lima Senior	75	Louisville	51
Mentor	62	East Liverpool	44

This final ranking was also a first with three Columbus-area teams in the UPI's Top 10 final rankings. It was ironic in that this tremendous success came after Coach Walker had considered leaving Watterson the year before, thinking of going to Warren Western Reserve and taking the head job there, being a product of John Carroll and knowing the area. But he changed his mind and stayed, much to the gratitude of thousands of Eagle fans. His team had finished 4th in 1965 with a 9-0 record, and his players could now brag in the malls and soda shops that they had a twenty-three-game streak going without a defeat, going through their '66 schedule by posting six shutouts and outscoring the opposition 350–40. But it isn't bragging if you've done it!

Coach Dick Walker later joined Ohio State and helped it to seven Big Ten titles through 1976 before joining the Pittsburgh Steelers for their Super Bowl seasons of 1978 and 1979. He died in 2013.

A 1966 "I Tried My Hardest" Story: Niles McKinley

As just described, Columbus Bishop Watterson won the championship in 1966, with Niles McKinley coming in as runner-up. What is forgotten about this year for most, except for those in Niles, is that this amazing team went undefeated at 10-0 and whipped Canton McKinley, Massillon and Warren G. Harding, the only Ohio team to ever do so in the same season. In comparison to their 1961 and 1963 state titles, this 1966 schedule was much more challenging.

Playing in a reconditioned stadium expanded by more than four thousand seats, the 1966 team would send twenty-two lettermen into battle. One of the great highlights of this season was ending Massillon's thirty-two-game winning streak, 20–12, in front of more than fifteen thousand crazy fans on the Red Dragons' turf. This satisfying win gained a measure of revenge for the Tigers' ending of Niles's own forty-eight-game win streak in 1964.

Coach Bob Shaw had taken charge of the Red Dragons team two years earlier from Tony Mason, the coach who had won two state titles earlier in the '60s and had moved on to college coaching. In an interview, Shaw expounded on the importance of football to the Niles community, noting that the emotions were so high that if you lost a game you would risk getting your house egged or wake up the next morning to "For Sale" signs in your front yard.

Going into the last game of the season, Niles thought it had it made, but after its capstone tenth win of the season, the team ended up second to Watterson, which had leapfrogged other teams to snag the title despite Niles having more 1st-place votes. Total votes were in Watterson's favor. In a hugely successful season with three singular wins against perennial powers, giving it all they had all season long, the Red Dragons came in second best.

No One Beat Us Either: Louisville

If you weren't paying attention to the Ohio Top 10 in 1966, you might have missed another great story of a team who had somewhat quietly built a three-year football record as good as Massillon, Niles or any other Ohio team.

Located in Stark County, the home of numerous high school football powers and just east of Canton, Ohio, the Louisville Leopards began playing football in 1924. Beginning in 1962, the Leopards started on a march to a 48-1-1 record through the 1966 season, ranking 5th in 1964's AP Poll ahead of the likes of Sandusky and Upper Arlington. That year, with leaders like Bob Gladieux, Mark Stier and twin brothers Tom and Mike Chlebeck, just about each game was perfect, with the Leopards achieving six shutouts, the closest game of the ten being a 38–12 win against North Canton. Gladieux went on to Notre Dame, and many others went to major schools like Ohio State, Syracuse, Cincinnati and others. For some reason, despite 10-0 records in 1965 and '66, they were not ranked in the AP Top 10 and only 9th in the UPI. To me, this placement speaks to the overall quality of football being played then.

The Leopards continued to be successful in the decades following this run, enduring the usual ups and downs, but this '60s string of wins had created something special that succeeding teams would build on and measure themselves against.

Marion Catholic High School

In 1965, the Ohio High School Athletic Association divided its high schools into two classes (A and AA) to establish a more even playing field for schools of all sizes. Marion Catholic High School in Marion, Ohio, was put into Class A, and it won the state title that year, going undefeated. It was not totally unexpected, as the team had also done well in '64. It's always about winning the next one that is interesting, especially if it is the very next year.

Coach Max Ross of Marion Catholic High School in Marion, Ohio, was entering the 1966 high school football season on a high, having won a state high school championship the year before and currently surfing the crest of a sixteen-game winning streak. The Fighting Irish of the small parochial school alongside Mount Vernon Avenue on Marion's east side had gone undefeated in 1965 under Ross and quarterback Mike Piacentino, winning the first state football championship in the city since the Harding High School Presidents won the UPI crown in 1958 (tying with the Alliance Aviators, who had won the AP vote). The Irish were strong once again, and the expectations that simmered over the summer of 1966 were that they could repeat, even though Piacentino was gone, off to Notre Dame University in South Bend, Indiana. The Irish had won three straight Mid-Ohio Conference championships and were favored for a fourth despite Piacentino and other key players graduating. But Coach Ross would have to see what this current incarnation was made of before echoing those sentiments.

The Irish opened the 1966 season on September 9 with a game played in Massillon Stadium against Dover St. Joseph, 1965's AP state champion. Both teams had finished 9-0 and had been voted state champions, Marion Catholic by the UPI. It was a game that would put any lingering questions about who deserved it more to rest. Their game would be the first game of a double-header played that day in Massillon. The game started at 5:30 p.m. Massillon time, that town being on Daylight Saving Time. The Tuscarawas

Valley High School Marching Band would represent Marion Catholic at the game, and two buses from Marion to carry fans there had been chartered. The Irish were going to stay at the Massillon Inn after the game and tour the Pro Football Hall of Fame on Saturday before returning home.

The game with Dover St. Joseph in front of fifteen thousand estimated fans was everything you would have expected from two teams who each had claimed a share of the state title the year before. It was a defensive battle, as befitting the season's first game, and the initial score was made by the Irish when Dennis Kapcar intercepted a pass and raced 35 yards for the touchdown. Coach Ross called a run to try for the two points, but they were stopped, so with 6:33 left in the first quarter, it was Marion Catholic ahead by six points.

Dover came out after the half and recovered a fumble on a flip made between Irish quarterback Dave Barbier and back Tim Grady. The rushing attempt was being made from the 3, and the ball was recovered in the end zone by Dover's Jeff Lammers, a senior linebacker. Their try for two points was also stopped.

Dover had an All-Ohio candidate at quarterback that year, Dave Myers, and with four seconds left in the third quarter and backed up to their end zone, he took a bad snap out of the shotgun that got by him. Tim Grady fell on it for a safety. It was a defensive slugfest after that, with each team unable to score again.

It was an 8–6 victory, and Ross praised his defensive unit for putting up a tremendous effort against a very strong offense. Next up would be Bucyrus next Friday at their place.

The Irish "had a thing going" with the Redmen of Bucyrus—for two years Catholic had finished 8-1, and each time that defeat had come at the hands of Bucyrus. The Irish had beaten them the year before, however, en route to their undefeated and state championship season, getting a heavy monkey off their back. The team had come through the Dover game unscathed and had good practices that week, so Coach Max Ross pronounced his team ready.

Bucyrus had won its first battle too, beating Tiffin Calvert, 13–0. Coach Bob Boyles thought that his team was ready to give the Irish a good game when they got there.

The Irish might have had some "bus lag" from their trip to Massillon the week before because by halftime of the Bucyrus contest they were down, 13–0, with the Redmen taking the ball right down the field the first time they had it and making it 7–0 just like that. On a subsequent series, the Irish attempted to air it out, and it was picked off by Mel Slaughter, a six-foot

170-pound junior defensive back, who took it down the sideline 35 yards for the TD. Slaughter was the only starter for the Redmen who was not a letterman! A run for the two points was stopped.

The Irish got the ball after receiving the kick, and after a few gains of three yards each, Tim Grady received the handoff and quickly got past the defense for a 59-yard scoring run. He went around right end for the two points and it was 13–8. Coach Ross took his team into the locker room at halftime and told them what they had to do, and they came back out and did it.

The Irish got it going in the second half and were leading, 24–13, when Bucyrus got one more try to make it in but failed thanks to the tough Irish defense.

The laudatory comments from the Bucyrus side were many and positive, while Coach Ross praised the way both the offense and defense responded to his halftime adjustments. He felt that they dominated the second half and said, "We beat them physically." Tim Grady had an outstanding game, scoring twice and making three two-point conversions.

The Mid-Ohio Conference slate of games was to begin that week, and Marion Catholic's first conference game would be against the Barons of Buckeye Valley, a team standing at 2-0 but also one the Irish had whipped the last three times they played them.

In a performance that set him on track for All-Ohio honors, Tim Grady, the Irish senior fullback, ran for 199 yards in thirty-one carries in carrying his team to an 18–6 conference win. He also excelled at middle linebacker throughout the game. It was the nineteenth straight win over three seasons for Catholic and the twenty-third consecutive conference victory.

This year's "Game of the Year" for the Irish was against the Cardington Pirates, a tough team from Morrow County who always gave the Irish a black-and-blue battle. The Pirates had won their first three games by wide margins, and Coach Kent Reed's squad was supremely confident coming to Marion to face the Marion Catholic boys. Coach Ross was just as confident and said that his guys were ready. In the ten years prior, the Pirates had won four, lost five and tied one, so they were not awed by the Irish and considered them a rival, pointing each year to this game as a big one.

Coach Ross mentioned Tim Grady that week, calling him "one of the most outstanding backs I've ever seen" and noting that he had gained 437 yards already for an average of 147 per game; he also gave credit to Dunn and Kapcar for clearing the way for his great running back.

The *Marion Star* noted in its report of the game that "both teams displayed bone-jarring tackling from the opening kickoff." It was so tough that the Irish held the Pirates to just 5 net rushing yards! Conversely, the Pirates held the Irish twice on short-yardage fourth-down plays in the fourth quarter. The only score came in the second quarter when on a third and 14 on the Catholic 36 Cusick shot through a hole and went 34 yards to the Cardington 30. Joe Whelan, an outstanding up-and-coming back, went for 2 yards, and then Tim Grady went up the middle and got loose and took it in for the score. Tim then took a pitchout from Barbier and went across for the two points.

Cardington felt that its own mistakes beat them, and Coach Ross felt that he did not coach very well, gambling too much on some plays. In any event, the Irish remained undefeated and had escaped with no serious injuries.

The polls that were released the following week were interesting. The UPI ranked Marion Catholic in 1st place with 129 points, with 2nd-place Millersport garnering only 61. Dover St. Joseph, last year's AP champ, which had been beaten by the Irish this year in the first game of the year, was ranked seventh at 2-2.

Oddly, the AP did not publish a poll that week for the Class A teams, citing a lack of participation among the sports writers and broadcasters. According to reports, only five or six ballots were cast for Class A!

The Olentangy Braves at 1-2-1 overall were the next opponent for the Irish on the Olentangy field. While Coach Ross would go with his normal backfield of the Grady brothers, Barbier and Cusick, Joe Whelan was also expected to see a lot of action.

Like any no. 1 team, those who played them seemed always to bring their best games, at least for some of the game. Such was the case in the game against Olentangy. Starting out slow, the Irish exploded for four touchdowns in the last three quarters to whip the Braves, 28–3. Tim Grady continued to impress everyone in the state as he juked and jived for 181 yards, completely "outshining the rest of the field" according to his coach. He scored twice and his brother, Kevin, once, along with Barbier and Whelan getting a PAT. This win made the Irish 5-0 and 4-0 in the conference.

The AP finally got enough of its group to vote in the Class A division, and the next week it had the Irish in front of Millersport, 69 points to 38. River Valley High School, another Marion County team, was voted no. 10. Dover St. Joseph, now 3-2, was voted in at no. 8. Marion Catholic was also still in the top spot in the UPI, 204 to 111, for Millersport. Mount Gilead, 4-1 overall and undefeated in the Mid-Ohio Conference, was next up for the Irish. The series record in the past ten years was 8-2 in favor of Marion Catholic.

Injuries are never good, and there is never a good time for them to happen or a good type to incur. They are especially troubling when they happen to your better players, and it is always a test for the coaches and the players to overcome the loss of such a player. Thus, the aftermath of the Mount Gilead game would be a test of character and strength.

Tim Grady suffered a fracture of his left leg in two places on the first play of the second quarter. He had already gained 117 yards and scored once and had just scooted 68 yards to set up the second. John Coning of Mount Gilead had caught Grady at the 9-yard line, and Grady was unable to get up. He was carried off the field to the bench, where he was still fighting desperately to stand but was unable to. X-rays at Marion General hospital showed clean breaks of the tibia and fibula, and he would be out for six weeks at least.

Kevin Brady, Tim's brother, moved into his spot, and sophomore Joe Whelan stepped in to take over Kevin's spot at halfback. The Irish went on that night to secure a 22–0 victory, but the mood was bittersweet in the locker room afterward. Coach Ross praised his defense and expressed shock at losing Tim Grady, who was running unmolested toward All-Ohioan honors until this horrible twist of fate. But the team promised to work all the harder to compensate for the loss of such a superior athlete.

The polls the following week showed the Irish maintaining their lead in the Associated Press by just one point, 100 to 99 over Millersport.

Practices after the Grady injury and in preparation for their game against Big Walnut were good according to Max Ross, with the players adapting to some personnel changes on both sides of the ball to maintain the skill level Grady had brought to the game. Beating Highland would bring to the Irish their twenty-third straight win and twenty-ninth consecutive victory in the Mid-Ohio Conference.

Responding as only champions do, the Marion Catholic gridders bombed Big Walnut, 46–0, in an inspirational win, amassing 434 yards on the ground in driving through the defense of Big Walnut like Patton and the Third Army through the Germans in World War II. Barbier scored three touchdowns, with Cusick, K. Grady and Kapcar one each.

In the ups and downs of the polling, where opinions vary like the weather, the Irish were still in 1st place in the AP, but this time the voting was 119 to 97 for second-place Millersport. No. 1 in the UPI as well (43 points above Millersport), the Irish prepared to play Highland for their annual Homecoming event. River Valley, also undefeated, was seeking its eighth in a row against Logan Hills.

Highland was pitiful in 1966, having won one game, and the expectations for the Marion Catholic's Homecoming game was a win, a big one, and solidification of its hold on the no. 1 place in both polls. The night before, River Valley in Marion County had destroyed Logan Hills, 53–0, and if it hadn't been evident before, there was some pretty good football going on in Marion County in 1966—and it wasn't just the school on Mount Vernon Avenue that was showing it. There was a lot riding on this game for the Irish, aside from the bragging rights of the county: it would guarantee the Irish a tie for first place in the conference; a win would certainly place them in position to win a second straight state championship with one game to go; and a win would get Max Ross the record for most straight wins in the Columbus Diocesan area—they were currently tied with Lancaster Fenwick. Plus, it was Homecoming, and all the guys wanted to win for their dates so the dance after the game would be a happy one.

Joe Whelan, a sophomore halfback, had been impressive in the times he had gotten in to play, showing much promise and ability. As any kid playing high school sports would tell you, given a chance they could shine. Well, the football gods shined their light on Joe the second from last game of the season in 1966.

There was just 7:07 left to play in the game, and up to that point the Irish had run into a Scottie buzz saw. The first two times the Irish had gotten the ball, they had not done a thing with it. Then, after a Highland punt taken at their 37, they started moving. Kevin Grady was stopped for no gain, and the Irish were penalized 5 yards back to their 33. Dave Barbier then threw a pass to Whelan at the 40 who outran the Scottie defense 67 yards for the TD. Kevin Grady took it in for the two points. On the first play of the second quarter, Highland's quarterback, Bill Irvine, passed to Don Davidson for a TD and then tried to pass for the two points, but Kevin Grady and Dave Barbier broke it up. Keith Cusick scored for the Irish later after Dennis Kapcar recovered a Highland fumble, caused by a crushing hit by Kapcar and Tom Dunn.

In the third quarter Whelan contributed on defense when he batted down a touchdown pass in the end zone after Highland had moved the ball downfield, with the Highland receivers making spectacular catches between Irish defenders. The Irish tried to move in the fourth quarter but were stymied, Barbier being dropped a few times. The Scotties scored again when Irvine followed 287-pound Dave Baker into the end zone. Whelan knocked down the two-point pass try, and the score was 16–12. No one watching this game was sitting down! One game to go and one more game to win and they would be state champs, but they had to rid themselves of these pesky Scotties from Highland!

The kick to Joe Whelan was high and looked rather like it was arching in slow motion, the light reflecting off the hide of the ball, the thing taking its own good time coming down to his waiting hands. He caught it at the 24 and started up the middle of the field; behind three outstanding blocks he broke into the open at the 50, and that was all she wrote. Joe was not touched by Highland players, and he sprinted across the goal line, smiling the adrenalin smile of a young guy making good! Kevin Grady tried to get across for the two but was brought down. He made up for that a few minutes later when after only two plays he intercepted a Highland throw at the 43 and brought it a few yards closer by moving it to the 48. After a twelve-play drive, Kevin took it over from the 6. The biggest gain in the drive was a 12-yard pass to Joe Whelan. It was his night.

Highland got close again, but Grady intercepted a pass at the goal line. However, interference was called, and they got another chance at scoring. But it was incomplete, and the Marion Catholic footballers got their win.

The AP Poll the following week boosted their lead to 143 points to a lagging Millersport at 115, a six-point increase over the previous week. River Valley, the other undefeated Marion County team, was in a tie for 16th.

In the *Marion Star* that week, it was said that this week was the moment of truth for Marion Catholic High School: could they win that one last game, maintain their spot at the top and win a second straight state championship? That last game, against North Union High School, was the decider all right. Could a team who had averaged 22.7 points a game against an average of 5.6 for their opponents keep it up one last time? Could a team who had lost its star player do it one more time?

Well, Coach Ross thought they could. He said that week, "We've went a long way for the 1966 Class A state championship and we are not going to be denied at this point." Following Saturday's game, the Irish would make a short visit to the St. Mary convent and then downtown to the courthouse for a rally, win or lose.

Eight seniors were slated to play their final game for Marion Catholic against North Union on Saturday night. A pep rally was planned for Friday at 6:30 p.m., including a bonfire and introductions of the players and coaches. The Irish would be shooting for their twenty-fifth straight victory and their thirty-first in the conference. But that week snow was the big story, with large accumulations everywhere in central Ohio and the cancelation of several games, forcing indoor practices in some cases, including North Union retreating inside on Wednesday. Some games were postponed to the following

Monday, including some in Marion County. Totals of six to ten inches of snow were discussed by the local weather experts for different parts of the surrounding counties. Whatever the accumulations, it would affect gameplay.

The home game at Harding's field was kind of in doubt up to the last minute because of the snow. Coach Ross, after inspecting the field Friday morning, made the call to play the game.

John Short of the *Marion Star* wrote in the first paragraph of his report of this game that "a touchdown in the final 10 seconds of the first half and another with just over two minutes left in the game carried Marion Catholic's Fighting Irish to a 12–0 victory over a determined North Union team here Saturday night."

Coach Ross afterward cited co-captains Tim Grady and Kevin Dunn as keys to that year's success. "They were great leaders," he said. "They had a tremendous job to do in molding this team. But last August they came in shape, they came ready to play, and they exerted the leadership."

The River Valley game against Ridgedale, held on the following Monday because of the heavy snows, was also a victory and left the Vikings undefeated as well, their 38–0 victory very impressive.

The AP Poll following the Irish win showed the voters lowering the margin of Catholic's lead to 114 points, 29 fewer than the previous week. Millersport was in second at 104. River Valley climbed to the 11th spot in a solid and very gratifying showing to all in Marion County.

The polls released on November 11 showed Marion Catholic in 1st place in both polls, thereby winning the state championship unequivocally. Not a divided championship this time—this time everybody agreed!

Marion Catholic High School, a small parochial school in Marion, Ohio, stands as equals with the teams of Stark County, the Cleveland and Cincinnati teams and other teams who have had their moment of glory as state champions in the best football state in the nation. Its kids were as tough and focused as any anywhere, and there should be no hesitation when talking of them in the same breath as those teams.

Max Ross would retire from coaching to enter private business at the end of the 1967 season. That year, he suffered an 8–8 tie with North Union in the season's last game and lost the Mid-Ohio Conference crown for the first time since 1963. The tie also ended a thirty-six-game winning streak in the conference that harkened back to 1962. Ross was only forty years old and ended his career at 55-14-3, for a .764 winning percentage. He was twice named Coach of the Year in Ohio, in 1965 and 1966, his championship years.

All hail Marion Catholic!

1967

Upper Arlington is a well-heeled suburb of Columbus, Ohio, located on high ground between the Olentangy and Scioto Rivers. The community was conceived and founded in 1913 by two real estate developers who wanted to call the area "Country Club District," but it became known as Upper Arlington due to its relation to Columbus of Arlington just south of it. The layout of the streets and the architecture of the homes gave it a village type of atmosphere, with landed manor estates that attracted the affluent Buckeye families of the day.

To add to the desirable aspects of this lovely place is the school system, begun in 1924 and now ranked as one of the best in both the state and the nation, as well as having some of the best facilities in the area. The high school's sports programs have produced some of the best teams in the central Ohio area and continually vie for championships in all sports. The school began its football program in 1926, having won more than forty Ohio Athletic Association State Championships, winning the football title in 1967, 1968, 1969 and 2000. The Summer of Love in 1967 seemingly had little impact on the fitness program the Golden Bears of Coach Marv Moorhead were going through to get ready for their opener against Lancaster.

The 1967 version of the Upper Arlington football team was not a bunch with extensive game experience, but there were a few skilled players hanging around from the year before, when they lost their only game to eventual state champ Bishop Watterson. Graduation had taken some good players away, but the reserve program in UA was exceptional, and they seemed to reload instead of fretting about their seniors moving on.

They started out with that single loss still fresh in their minds and were still a little too emotional about it, not moving the ball against Lancaster and making mistakes, but they eventually got their grounding and started scoring easily, coming away with a 46–22 victory on September 8. Dave Gordon and Gary Moore each scored twice, and three other Golden Bears crossed the goal line for six points.

Upper Arlington was ranked fifth in the UPI and sixth in the AP at the end of 1966 and was intent on bettering that standing in 1967. It did so by wearing down its opponents via a steamroller offense and hard-hitting defense. But it took a while to get cranking against South in the second game, as it was only 13–6 at the end of the first half. But the Golden Bears scored the first time they got the ball in the second half and never looked back, scoring thirteen points in the third quarter and nineteen in the last, making it a 45–6 shellacking. Geoff Schmidt scored three touchdowns for Upper Arlington. A defensive highlight for the Golden Bears was a Denny Dickie interception (one of two), returning it for a 43-yard touchdown. This game was also the last of a twenty-three-game series that Upper Arlington had played with South. Across town, the defending Class AA state champion, Watterson, was defeated by Linden-McKinley, 22–12, to end the Eagles' twenty-game winning streak and set the hunt for the 1967 crown wide open.

In the first UPI Poll, released on September 19 (1st-place votes in parenthesis), Upper Arlington was 5th with the first four in order being: Canton McKinley (13), Sandusky High School (5), Massillon Washington (1) and Steubenville (4). The Golden Bears received two 1st-place votes and 120 points to Canton McKinley's 238 points for 1st place. Upper Arlington was leading in central Ohio with 91 points scored against 28 given up.

The Golden Bears were thus primed for their first home game of the year, against Springfield South of the Greater Ohio League. Relying on a balanced attack, the offense gained 222 yards rushing and 202 yards passing with the state champion in the 440-yard dash, Denny Dickie, leading the ground guys with 80 yards in twelve tries. Quarterbacks Scott Stanley and Ted McNulty hit on seventeen of thirty-one via the air and four touchdowns as the Bears whipped the Wildcats, 54–0, and sent them home whimpering! Scoring by quarters was very consistent at 14, 13, 14 and 13.

In the Associated Press poll released on September 26, 1967, Upper Arlington moved up to 3rd place in Double A. Canton McKinley was still no. 1, and Massillon Washington was next. Point totals for those three teams were 172, 127 and 119, respectfully, with Steubenville nipping at the Golden Bears in 4th with 114 points. 5th-place Cincinnati Roger Bacon was very distant at only 54 points in the voting.

In the UPI voting that week, the UA Golden Bears were 4th, with the top three teams being Canton McKinley, Massillon Washington and Steubenville—in 5th stood Roger Bacon. Canton McKinley had 313 points and Upper Arlington 178. Clearly the Golden Bears had some ground to make up to snag the no. 1 spot.

Well, they did. The Golden Bears romped over Newark, 32–0, in the fourth game of the season as they gained 387 yards rushing and 94 yards via the pass. Gary Moore, the senior halfback for Coach Moorhead's offensive machine, carried thirteen times for 209 yards and took in two passes for 26 yards while scoring two TDs.

The October 3 AP Poll showed Canton McKinley still in the lead, Massillon in 2nd (although they barely got by the Alliance Aviators, 20–14) and Upper Arlington in 3rd place, but only a single point in front of the Big Red of Steubenville. Steubenville had crushed Warren Harding the previous Friday, 40–12, for its fourth straight victory. However, things were different in the UPI; there, the Big Red jumped to 2nd place behind Canton McKinley, with Massillon Washington 3rd and the Golden Bears in 4th. Cincinnati Roger Bacon was just a point behind Upper Arlington. The press was already talking about the upcoming clash of the titans between Massillon Washington and Upper Arlington on October 20 in Massillon!

First, though, the Golden Bears had to travel on October 6 to Mount Vernon. The Yellow Jackets were outclassed from the start by the Golden Bears and gave Coach Marv Moorhead his ninetieth victory with a 54–7 virtually uncontested win. It was a complete route, with Upper Arlington getting everyone who traveled that night into the game. The coach thought that his team "was improving with every game."

Tuesday, October 10, showed Upper Arlington in the 2nd-place position behind Canton McKinley in the AP Poll, but only by 14 points. This was based on the strength of the Golden Bears' win and a narrow Steubenville 14–6 win over Canton Lincoln. Massillon Washington dropped to 3rd. In the UPI, it was Canton McKinley, Steubenville, Massillon Washington, Upper Arlington and Cincinnati Roger Bacon. McKinley was to entertain Steubenville that coming Friday in a huge game, with that UA-Massillon game coming in the next week. This was shaping up as one of the best seasons in Ohio high school football for many years.

On Friday, October 13, UA entertained Bishop Ready of the Central Catholic League and won easily, 37–6. Geoff Schmidt scored on runs of 2, 4 and 2 yards, while Ted McNulty hit halfback Gary Moore for touchdown passes of 26 and 18 yards. It was 24–0 at the half, but the Bears were held scoreless in the third quarter before scoring 14 in the fourth. Upper Arlington was now 6-0 and had scored 268 points while holding the opposition to 41.

It was a huge night for the Steubenville Big Red of Coach Abe Ryan as they galloped 85 yards in the last minute to beat Canton McKinley to win, 20–15, securing the game on a tipped pass by the McKinley defenders in their end zone into the hands of halfback Keith Burke in one of the most thrilling games in Ohio high school history. Canton McKinley had been in the top spot all season, but when the polls came out Tuesday, October 17, the Big Red were ranked no. 1 in both, with Massillon Washington 2nd and the Golden Bears in 3rd place. In the AP, Bacon was 4th and McKinley 5th, while in the UPI Toledo St. Francis was 5th and McKinley 6th. That week, UA headed north to play the undefeated Tigers in the most hallowed stadium in Ohio.

Paul Horning wrote in the *Columbus Dispatch* that week that "it wouldn't be too surprising if the giant Kodiak bear in the entrance hall to Upper Arlington High School began snarling and flailing his way out of the glass 'cage' by Friday afternoon."

Some four thousand fans were estimated to have made the trip to Massillon on October 20, and they witnessed a game to be remembered for a long time. Scoreless after the first quarter, the Tigers scored in the second on an interception by fleet-footed Marc Malinowski at the Tigers' 21-yard line, and he went the 70 yards for the TD, aided by good blocking from the alert defense. The conversion failed: 6–0.

With 9:11 left in the last quarter, the Golden Bears started a drive from their own 28. Geoff Schmidt carried eight times, Scott Stanley passed for two first downs and Gary Moore made a first down on a fourth and six. UA got to the Tigers' 2-yard line, where Schmidt bulled over with 4:46 left. Scott Huston, the Bears' place kicker, booted one straight and high for the winning extra point with the aid of determined protection from his linemen. Upper Arlington wins, 7–6.

The Golden Bears had nineteen first downs to the Tigers' eight and had 240 total rushing yards to the home team's 179, losing only 11 and showing

All-American Ted McNulty of UA chases down Massillon's Will Foster. *Courtesy UA Archives and Upper Arlington School District.*

all that they could run as well as this vaunted Stark County powerhouse. Geoff Schmidt led all runners with 108 very hard-earned yards in thirty-one carries. Gary Moore had 81. Arlington totaled 144 more yards and eleven more first downs than Massillon.

Coach Moorehead had effusive praise for his defense. In a dreadful turn, however, he himself was injured when a runner kicked him in his leg running out of bounds, with the leg swelling tremendously, but this hardly dampened his enthusiasm over the win. Coach Seaman of Massillon commented after the game, "Wish I had to get ready for only one game a year instead of 10. We play too darn many tough ones." A little sour grapes, maybe?

In other action, no. 1 Steubenville barely won, 14–0, over Coach Forrest Sharrock's Stallions of Columbus DeSales. The Big Red scored their fourteen points in the first quarter but were then severely outplayed by the 1-5 Columbus team, outgaining Steubenville 252-185 in yardage and picking up fourteen first downs to the Big Red's eight. It was not a good showing for the top-ranked team in Ohio.

Yet in the polls that Tuesday, October 24, Steubenville High School retained the no. 1 ranking, with the Golden Bears close behind, the AP point totals being 182-179 and the UPI 323-296. The biggest move was by Cincinnati Roger Bacon, which jumped to third place by virtue of its 45–0 Sunday afternoon pounding of the Queen City powerhouse Moeller High School and Massillon Washington's loss. Only four of the Top 10 teams retained their positions from the previous week. Coming up for Steubenville was a contest with Ohio River rival Weirton from neighboring West Virginia and a November 3 battle with Massillon Washington, and then the Big Red would end up with their own in-town rival, Steubenville Catholic, on the tenth. The Golden Bears had Worthington next, then Cambridge and then the 1966 state champions, Bishop Watterson of Columbus. Breathing down their necks was Roger Bacon and the rest of the Top 10.

Coach Moorehead did not make the Worthington game, getting treatment for the injured leg in Riverside Hospital in Columbus. But it didn't matter. No disrespect to this great coach, because the big Bears of Upper Arlington just demolished Worthington, 76–0, amassing 652 yards of offense in an aggressive showing of history-making proportions. Steubenville High School whipped Weirton, West Virginia, 32–19.

The October 31 polls showed no change in the top three teams, with the Big Red up against Massillon Washington in a replay of the previous year's match-up that cost them the state championship. Going into that game undefeated and untied, they lost to the Tigers, 12–0. It was not something they wanted to happen again, and preparations that week in Steubenville were intense to defeat the invading Massillon team coached by Bob Seaman. These two teams' series records were heavily in Washington's favor, the Tigers holding an edge at 26-3-1. In other games that weekend, losses were suffered by Toledo St. Francis (losing to Cleveland St. Joseph, 23–21) and Canton McKinley (bowing to Alliance, 21–14).

In one of those situations where you know something could happen and it does, it did that night when the Big Red and the Tigers met. Before a record crowd in Steubenville's Harding Stadium, the Tigers whipped the home team, 26–16 behind six-foot-four, 200-pound Washington halfback Jim Smith.

Two pass interceptions and a fumble recovery by Massillon in the last four minutes secured the victory and knocked the Big Red from the undefeated ranks. Meanwhile, down south, the Golden Bears of Upper Arlington creamed Cambridge, 47–0, before a screaming home crowd. Coach Moorhead was still in the hospital but due to be released that Sunday, but it was in the record books as his ninety-fourth win and the Bears' thirty-seventh in the last thirty-eight games.

As expected, the November 7 polls for 1967 had UA no. 1, followed by Massillon Washington, Roger Bacon, Steubenville and Dover in the AP, as well as Sandusky likewise in the UPI. In the AP, their margin over Massillon was 182-157 and, in the UPI, a very close 299-292. Clearly, the team had to continue their dominance to maintain these slim leads. It would be a repeat of 1966, when Upper Arlington was in 2nd place in the UPI poll heading into the Bishop Watterson match-up and had a chance for the top spot but was beaten. In a drama so many times played out in sports, this type of repeat situation made for an exciting and highly anticipated contest scheduled for November 10.

The *Columbus Dispatch* sports page of November 9 carried the headline of "Eagles Eye Spoiler Role" and quoted Watterson's rookie coach Ronnie Shay as saying that his Eagles would be "up and ready" for the Upper Arlington game. Reviewing his current team's 5-3-1 performance against the championship 10-0 year just twelve months removed, he noted that the players were jelling in the latter part of the season and were coming on strong after some early season injuries. About Upper Arlington, he said, "We have a few ideas as to where to hit them and we feel certain plays can crack their defense." The Watterson offense had thrown very little that year, and they ran a six-two defense, so they believed in smash-mouth hitting and strength as a football philosophy. It was to be tested the next night at 7:30 p.m.

It was a rainy night in Columbus that Friday, and those November rains in Ohio are generally cold and miserable to anyone venturing outside to pick up a gallon of milk let alone play football for tremendous stakes. Coach Moorhead, now in his thirteenth year at UA, was on the sidelines leaning on crutches from his injury a few weeks earlier. The 6,500 people watching the game in this dismal weather were the most diehard of fans and, along with the Watterson players, did not seem to mind the cold and the wet. It did seem to bother the Golden Bears, however, at least in the first half.

Watterson, playing emotional football, jumped off to a 12–0 lead thanks to some good running by John Motil, a 190-pound quarterback who liked to run around the ends. A fine passer as well, Motil skirted the Upper Arlington defense on a 61-yard scoot for the first touchdown of this dreary night. His pass for the two-point conversion was overthrown. Then, Watterson's Ed Warner recovered a fumble on the UA 20-yard line and after moving the ball to the 2-yard line, Bobby Boyd took it in with 5:58 remaining in the half. That was it for Watterson, and the second half turned out to be a new ballgame.

The Golden Bears scored thirty-one unanswered points in the second half and walked away with a victory and an assumed state championship. This game was a huge turning point in the Bears' history, capping off their third undefeated season in the past four years and the thirty-eighth victory out of the last thirty-nine games before Watterson did them in the year before.

The UA fans mobbed the locker room and chanted, "We're no. 1" after the game. Coach Moorhead was pulled into the shower and wetted down completely, bum leg and all. He said after, "I've been dunked before…but 12 points down and coming back with 31…that's the sweetest."

A year before, they had lost to this same school, 32–0, an extremely hurtful defeat that was remembered throughout the season and built on to this day. The coach said, "I've had great teams, but this 1967 bunch covered more ground and really grew up. They just like to hit.…We didn't have a bad game all season. Sure, we'd have a bad quarter, or maybe a half, but we always came back, and that's the mark of a great team."

An amazing photo in the November 11 *Columbus Dispatch*, which thoroughly covered this game, was that of Golden Bears coach Pete Corey atop a very tall ladder with a walkie-talkie observing the gameplay and communicating what he saw to the UA sidelines. This was done because there were no press box–to–field communication facilities in the Watterson stadium. The risks one takes for victory!

"Upper Arlington Nails High School Polls Title" was the sports page headline on Tuesday, November 14, 1967. The Associated Press showed it this way:

AP	Wins	Losses	Ties	Points
Upper Arlington	10	0	0	230
Massillon	9	1	0	203
Cincinnati Roger Bacon	10	0	0	185
Steubenville	9	1	0	131
Dover	10	0	0	108
Shelby	10	0	0	96
Sandusky	9	1	0	89
Circleville	10	0	0	70
Toledo St. Francis	8	1	0	42
Cincinnati Princeton	8	1	1	37

The UPI looked this way (1st place votes in parentheses):

UPI	Wins	Losses	Ties	Points
Upper Arlington (17)	10	0	0	390
Cincinnati Roger Bacon (10)	10	0	0	375
Massillon (10)	9	1	0	361
Steubenville (2)	9	1	0	286
Sandusky (4)	9	1	0	230
Lima Senior	7	2	0	96
Toledo St. Francis (1)	8	1	0	94
Shelby	10	0	0	87
East Liverpool (1)	9	1	0	81
Cincinnati Princeton	8	1	1	72

The UPI was a much closer call than the AP and contained several differences of opinion. That wire service thought much more of Roger Bacon and voted a 7-2 Lima Senior team into the Top 10, while the AP saw fit to include Dover and Circleville, two teams who did not appear in the UPI! Massillon Washington was deemed unsuitable to be no. 2 in the UPI but entirely suited for that spot in the AP. These differences go back to the imperfection of the polls, with their diverse opinions, regional beliefs and hit-and-miss geographical coverage of the many, many teams involved.

Four Upper Arlington players who were picked for the All-District squad: quarterback Brian Kitchen, center Tom Franklin, linebacker Duke Chandler and defensive tackle Denny Lawrence. Lawrence was named All-Ohio. *Courtesy Upper Arlington Public Library, UA Archives and Upper Arlington School District.*

Coach Marv Moorhead said, "We are pleased, to say the least. The kids are ecstatic. We had some really good players, but our strength lay in the fact they were a team in the finest sense of the word." Moorhead said he felt that 1967 was a rebuilding year after they lost heavily via graduation. But he said, "We never sold these kids short."

It was certainly the highlight of Coach Moorhead's seventeen-year career, a 1944 graduate of North High School in Columbus as well as the "Cradle of Coaches," Miami University, in 1951. He began as an assistant at Upper Sandusky and then moved to Eaton as head coach for two years before moving to Evanston High in Illinois as a line coach and then back to the Columbus area at UA.

At the traditional football banquet held at a local Sheraton Hotel, it just happened to be Coach Moorhead's fortieth birthday, and his parents were down from Marblehead, Ohio, to honor their son for his team's fantastic success. He noted that this year's defense was the best in the school's history, holding the opposition to just fifty-nine points, and added that the offense's yardage mark of 4,134 was comparable to the best college teams. Many players were honored, and co-captains for 1968 were announced as being Geoff Schmidt and Bruce Johnson. The coach was honored with a painting of a Golden Bear, and a large map of Ohio was displayed, adorned with ten stars representing the site of each victory.

Steubenville High School Big Red: Two Good Stories

The Steubenville High School Big Red finished the 1967 season ranked 4th in both the Double A AP and UPI Polls. They have a rich football history stretching back decades and always seemed to be in the polls somewhere.

Steubenville may have played football games as early as 1885, but the first significant and most everlasting event in its football résumé occurred in 1912, when a young man by the name of Charles Quidland "Punque" Cartledge graduated from Steubenville High School, where he had just finished being the captain of the football, basketball and baseball teams, going 6-1 in football as the quarterback. Four years later, he took over the job as head football coach for the first time (because he only stayed for the 1916 season and then went into the United States Army during World War I). He then returned for the 1919 season and started down a history-making road.

An awful lot has been written about Coach Cartledge, but not too much recently, and it is a shame because he deserves to be mentioned in the same breath as any of the top coaches to come out of Ohio at any level of football. At various times, he was described as a taskmaster, softhearted, a disciplinarian, an inventor and a second father to many of the boys he coached; in other words, he was an ideal person to coach high school football. During his tenure in Steubenville (1916, 1919–40), he won 133 games, lost 39 and tied 9. Coaches from many states and inside Ohio came to the town on the Ohio River to watch this man work his magic and learn his methods. One of them was Paul Brown, a man who will be mentioned many times in this history and who attributed much of his dynastic success at Massillon Washington High School to what he learned from Coach Cartledge. Knute Rockne also paid Punque top-notch accolades. Tributes don't come any better than that.

Steubenville was also home to many famous and controversial people, from Dean Martin to Jimmy "The Greek" Snyder, but the most interesting to me is that it was the birthplace of Dorothy Sloop Heflick, who, while no one knows for sure, is thought to have been the inspiration for the song "Hang On Sloopy" written by Wes Ferrell and Bert Russell. Heflick, who went by "Sloop," was a jazz pianist and singer who lived from 1913 to 1998 and toured with bands from the 1930s through the 1950s. She subsequently retired to Florida and became a teacher and died later in Mississippi.

"Hang On Sloopy" was recorded by the McCoys, a group from over in Dayton, for Bang Records, and the rest is history. The tune charted on August 14, 1965 and went to Billboard's Top 100 as no. 1 on October 2. A band member for the Ohio State Marching Band, John Tatgenhorst, liked it so much that he persuaded the band's director to play it, and it is now a Saturday OSU Buckeye tradition in the Horseshoe to play it before the start of the fourth quarter. It has become synonymous with hanging tough and not giving up.

Later, the 116th Ohio General Assembly designated "Hang On Sloopy" the state's official rock song by House Concurrent Resolution 16 on November 20, 1985. The complete resolution follows and is hilarious:

HOUSE CONCURRENT RESOLUTION NO. 16

WHEREAS, The members of the 116th General Assembly of Ohio wish to recognize the rock song "Hang On Sloopy" as the official rock song of the great State of Ohio; and

WHEREAS, In 1965, an Ohio-based rock group known as the McCoys reached the top of the national record charts with "Hang On Sloopy," composed by Bert Russell and Wes Farrell, and that same year, John Tatgenhorst, then an arranger for the Ohio State University Marching Band, created the band's now-famous arrangement of "Sloopy," first performed at the Ohio State–Illinois football game on October 9, 1965; and

WHEREAS, Rock music has become an integral part of American culture, having attained a degree of acceptance no one would have thought possible twenty years ago; and

WHEREAS, Adoption of "Hang On Sloopy" as the official rock song of Ohio is in no way intended to supplant "Beautiful Ohio" as the official state song, but would serve as a companion piece to that old chestnut; and

WHEREAS, If fans of jazz, country-and-western, classical, Hawaiian and polka music think those styles also should be recognized by the state, then by golly, they can push their own resolution just like we're doing; and

WHEREAS, "Hang On Sloopy" is of particular relevance to members of the Baby Boom Generation, who were once dismissed as a bunch of long-haired, crazy kids, but who now are old enough and vote in sufficient numbers to be taken quite seriously; and

WHEREAS, Adoption of this resolution will not take too long, cost the state anything, or affect the quality of life in this state to any appreciable degree, and if we in the legislature just go ahead and pass the darn thing, we can get on with more important stuff; and

WHEREAS, Sloopy lives in a very bad part of town, and everybody, yeah, tries to put my Sloopy down; and

WHEREAS, Sloopy, I don't care what your daddy do, 'cause you know, Sloopy girl, I'm in love with you; therefore be it Resolved, That we, the members of the 116ᵗʰ General Assembly of Ohio, in adopting this Resolution, name "Hang On Sloopy" as the official rock song of the State of Ohio; and be it further Resolved, That the Legislative Clerk of the House of Representatives transmit duly authenticated copies of this Resolution to the news media of Ohio.

Whether Steubenville's Dorothy Heflick really was the inspiration, it's a great story, and as the John Ford movie line goes, "When the legend becomes fact, print the legend."

1968

For the 1968 season, the Upper Arlington Golden Bears joined the Central Ohio League and won the state AA championship for the second straight year with a 10-0 record while establishing a record twenty straight victories.

The Canton McKinley Bulldogs, continuing their up-and-down decade, bounced back this year with a strong season and lost only to Niles McKinley, 16–0, beating the Massillon Washington Tigers in their traditional titanic struggle at the end, 26–6. They finished 3rd in the final AP Poll just ahead of Elyria.

Marion Motley, one of the Bulldogs' greatest alumni, was inducted into the Pro Football Hall of Fame this year. He had played for Paul Brown with the Cleveland Browns for many years and then later for the Pittsburgh Steelers in a comeback attempt as a linebacker. While in high school, he

Top: The 1968 Canton McKinley Bulldogs. *Courtesy Canton City Schools.*

Bottom: Canton McKinley versus Massillon, November 9, 1968. *Courtesy Canton City Schools.*

and the Bulldogs went 25-3, losing those few games to rival Massillon and Coach Paul Brown.

Coach Brown knew Motley well, and after Marion got out of the navy, where Coach Brown also coached him on its service team, he drafted him for the Browns. On the Navy team, Coach Brown created the draw play, a delayed handoff to Motley that took advantage of Marion's sprinter's speed and 240 pounds of muscle. Motley would burst through the line before the defenders knew what happened. This was another of many firsts that Paul Brown brought to the sport.

Brown would later write in his autobiography:

> *Motley became our greatest fullback ever because not only was he a great runner, but also no one ever blocked better—and no one ever cared more*

Above and right: Marion Motley as a Canton McKinley Bulldog. *Courtesy Canton City Schools*.

about his team and whether it won or lost, no matter how many yards he gained or where he was asked to run.…Marion's tremendous running ability also was what made our trap and draw plays so effective. When he ran off tackle, people seemed to fly off him in all directions. He possessed tremendous speed for a big man, and he could run away from linebackers and defensive backs when he got into the open—if he didn't trample them first. I've always believed that Motley could have gone into the Hall of Fame solely as a linebacker if we had used him only at that position. He was as good as our great ones.

When Marion was drafted by the Browns, they also brought in Bill Willis, and the two, along with Woody Strode and Kenny Washington (first to sign a contract) of the Los Angeles Rams, became the first African American players, all in 1946, in the professional All-America Football Conference (AAFC), later joining the new NFL in 1950. Encountering tortuous racism throughout their careers, they battled back by being exceptional on the field of play.

Elyria: Could Have Been

One of the best adjunct stories this year was about the Elyria Pioneers, ranked no. 4, who blitzed all comers but couldn't get the votes to get by the next three teams. There were no playoffs yet in Ohio—more's the pity—and one wonders, as we did most years, who the real champion could have been with a playoff scheme. The Pioneers had a run from 1968 to 1972 in which they lost just four games with three 10-0 seasons and four Buckeye

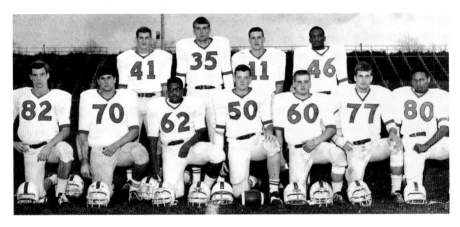

Top: The 1968 Elyria offense. *From the* Elyria Chronicle-Telegram.

Bottom: Elyria running back Tony Godbolt scores at Sandusky. *From the* Elyria Chronicle-Telegram.

The 1968 Elyria defense; its opponents only scored twenty-four points all year. *From the Elyria Chronicle-Telegram.*

Conference crowns, one of the top conferences in the state. I know, having played against these guys for three of those years, that Elyria would have matched up with anybody in the state on a man-to-man basis.

The 1968 Elyria High School football team was enshrined in the Elyria Sports Hall of Fame in 1996. Very definitely, they were tough guys and excellent football players.

Mentor High School Cardinals

Mentor High School up in Lake County jolted the state of Ohio by whipping Massillon, 19–0, on September 6, 1968—at Massillon, no less, in front of 13,290 fans who were probably expecting a summer outing and a happy ride home. Mentor used the win as motivation to fight to a 10-0 season and a final ranking of no. 2 behind Upper Arlington. Massillon finished 1968 at 7-3.

Dick Crum, the coach of the Cardinals, was another one of the many notable coaches Ohio high schools seemed to churn out annually. Playing his college football at Mount Union and Muskingum, he coached at Boardman, Sandusky and Warren Harding before coming in 1963 to Mentor, where he went 50-9-1 over six years. Following his 1969 season at Mentor, he took a job at Miami University. There he was an assistant coach under Bill Mallory, taking over as head coach in 1974. In four years as the Redskins' head coach, Crum posted a 34-10-1 record with three Mid-American Conference

Canton McKinley versus Massillon, November 9, 1968. *Courtesy Canton City Schools.*

championships and Tangerine Bowl victories over Georgia and South Carolina. He later coached North Carolina and Kent State. But September 6, 1968, is etched into his memory as one of the best.

The AP AA final poll for 1968 showed the Top 10 as:

1. Upper Arlington
2. Mentor
3. Canton McKinley
4. Elyria
5. Struthers
6. Warren Western Reserve
7. Shelby
8. Cleveland St. Joseph
9. Cincinnati St. Xavier
10. Warren Harding

1969

In 1969, the Upper Arlington Golden Bears extended their winning streak to thirty straight victories and won the league and state championships one more time, and their senior class was the first to never have been in a losing varsity football game. They were truly powerful football players. Doug Miller, Jeff Stark and Mark Zellmer were the tri-captains who led the Golden Bears through this amazing third-straight undefeated season, giving up only fifty-four points and never allowing an opponent to score an extra point. Twelve players from this team were elected to the All-COL team.

The AP AA final poll for 1969 in Ohio showed the Top 7 as:

1. Upper Arlington
2. Elyria
3. Cincinnati Moeller
4. Canton McKinley
5. Warren Western Reserve
6. Akron Garfield
7. Niles McKinley

The different looking UPI AA final poll for 1969 showed the Top 7 as:

1. Upper Arlington
2. Cincinnati Moeller
3. Elyria
4. Canton McKinley
5. Warren Western Reserve
6. Niles McKinley
7. Cleveland St. Joseph

Those teams following Upper Arlington in either poll could have had a shot at the title if the Golden Bears had stumbled. All were good teams and on any Friday night or Saturday afternoon, in some cases, could beat the others. Cincinnati Moeller, for instance, was a powerful squad coached by Gerry Faust, who later went on to coach Notre Dame. He felt that winning the Greater Cincinnati League "is like being number one in Ohio." He had a right to feel like that in 1969. Moeller had rolled over everyone it met and went undefeated at 10-0. Coach Faust would go to

Notre Dame after racking up a 178-23-2 high school record from 1960 through the 1980 season, winning five state championships.

Canton McKinley had a claim as well, beating Alliance, Massillon and Niles McKinley while suffering a single loss at Steubenville late in the season. After the Bulldogs beat them, 14–7, in the last game of the season before 22,200 fans on Saturday afternoon at Fawcett Stadium in Canton, many Massillon fans said that McKinley's eleven were possibly the best the school ever put on a field and should be no. 1 based on their tough schedule. They ended up no. 4 in both polls.

Elyria was again tough and rated serious consideration for the top spot. It was no. 2 in the AP and no. 3 in the UPI and once again never found enough votes to get to no. 1.

The Upper Arlington Golden Bears of 1967, '68 and '69 were guys from a great selection of kids today called baby boomers, who came together at the right school at the right time under the right coach. Take one or two players away, move the time a year earlier or later or maybe move Coach Moorhead somewhere else, and all of this might not have happened. As it was, the stars were aligned for those three years in Upper Arlington, the likes of which are rarely seen and which must be recorded as historic. To describe these three

Canton McKinley versus Massillon, November 8, 1969. *Courtesy Canton City Schools.*

years as fate, kismet or karma could be right, but Coach Moorehead would probably say something like, "These kids were hitters—they all loved to hit, and they were a team first, a heck of a team."

There were several All-Ohioans from these teams, including Bruce Tetirick, placekicker, 1969, Harvard University; Alan Starr, linebacker, 1969, University of Kentucky; Dan Allender, tackle, 1969, Ohio Wesleyan University; James Merrell, end, 1968, Indiana University; Ted McNulty, quarterback, 1968, Indiana University; Douglas Crim, guard, 1968, Harvard University; and Stephen Sikora, tackle/def end, 1967, Princeton University. McNulty and Sikora were also high school All-Americans. Their winning streak stopped at forty-two games in 1971, but the Golden Bears would continue to be in the hunt for the state title nearly every year (winning it again in 2000, going 15-0 in their best season ever) and continue to produce All-Ohioans and major college football stars.

Coach Moorehead died in 1997, and the Marv Moorehead Stadium at Upper Arlington High School is named to honor his memory.

Quick Notes

Coach Bill Barton of Elyria was named UPI Coach of the Year, beating Marv Moorehead, Cincinnati Moeller's Jerry Faust and Norwalk St. Paul's Mike Gottfried.

In 1970, still undefeated for the fourth season in a row, the Golden Bears lost out to the Massillon Washington Tigers, finishing 2nd in the AP voting. Why? New voters, maybe. Or tired of Upper Arlington or maybe just missing Massillon? I could offer a conspiracy theory take here (how could a three-time champion go through another undefeated season, the team's fourth, and not be voted no. 1?), but it would be worthless. It just shows why the need for a playoff system manifested itself, and that vote may have contributed to why the expansion to more divisions and the number of teams participating was made. Ohio went to a playoff system in 1972.

Elyria was no. 2 in the AP Poll in 1971 at 10-0.

ASSOCIATED PRESS	UNITED PRESS INTERNATIONAL
1950: All Classes: Massillon	Massillon
1951: All Classes: Massillon	Massillon
1952: All Classes: Massillon	Massillon

Steubenville Big Red versus Canton McKinley. The Bulldogs got beat, 20–14. *Courtesy Canton City Schools.*

ASSOCIATED PRESS	UNITED PRESS INTERNATIONAL
1953: All Classes: Massillon	Massillon
1954: All Classes: Massillon	Massillon
1955: All Classes: Canton McKinley	Canton McKinley
1956: All Classes: Canton McKinley	Canton McKinley
1957: All Classes: Cleveland Benedictine	Cleveland Benedictine
1958: All Classes: Alliance	Marion Harding
1959: All Classes: Massillon	Massillon
1960: All Classes: Massillon	Massillon
1961: All Classes: Massillon	Niles McKinley
1962: All Classes: Toledo Central Cath	Toledo Central Catholic
1963: All Classes: Niles McKinley	Niles McKinley
1964: All Classes: Massillon	Massillon
1965: Class AA: Massillon; Class A: Dover St. Joseph	Sandusky & Marion Catholic

ASSOCIATED PRESS	UNITED PRESS INTERNATIONAL
1966: Class AA: Cols. Watterson; Class A: Marion Catholic	Watterson & Marion Catholic
1967: Class AA: Upper Arlington; Class A: Portsmouth Notre Dame	Upper Arlington & Portsmouth
1968: Class AA: Upper Arlington; Class A: Newark Cath	Upper Arlington & Newark Catholic
1969: Class AA: Upper Arlington; Class A: Norwalk St. Paul	Upper Arlington & Norwalk St. Paul

"HOW GOOD *IS* OHIO HS FOOTBALL?" AND OTHER THOUGHTS

I s Ohio high school football held to a higher quality or standard? Ohio's high-quality high school football can be attributed to several key factors. Early on, Ohio assembled a superior infrastructure of schools, conferences, officials and organizations that produced great teams and players. The state's industrial base drew a large population that spawned large, well-funded schools and kids with blue-collar work ethics. From its inception, professional football proliferated here with professional and semiprofessional teams throughout the state producing legendary stars and then filtered downward to the secondary schools. These factors all require extensive research and deserve books of their own. However, the following statistics highlight some of the unique aspects of Ohio high school football, and you can draw your own conclusions.

	Schools	Participation
Texas	1,069	163,922
California	1,017	97,079
Florida	602	43,515
Illinois	544	42,682
Ohio	699	42,490

Compiled by the National Federation of State High School Associations (http://www.nfhs.org).

ALL-TIME WINS OF OHIO HIGH SCHOOLS

All-Time Wins	School	State	Data
871	Massillon Washington	OH	(1894–2017, 871-290-36)
828	Canton McKinley	OH	(1894–2017, 828-352-42)
806	Steubenville	OH	(1900–2017, 806-316-36)
700	Martins Ferry	OH	(1907–2017, 699-372-36)
691	Fostoria	OH	(1896–2017, 691-458-42)
688	Dover	OH	(1896–2017, 686-360-44)

Compiled by the National Federation of State High School Associations (http://www.nfhs.org).

In all-time wins by a school nationally, only Kentucky (ten) and Pennsylvania (eleven) have more schools ranked in total wins than Ohio. Other states have two schools or fewer in the top echelon.

TOP 5 ALL-TIME WINS

All-Time Wins	School	State	Data
911	Valdosta	GA	(1913–17; 1919-2017, 911-227-34)
885	Fort Thomas Highlands	KY	(1915–2017, 885-237-26)
878	Louisville Male	KY	(1893–2017, 878-328-49)
873	Mayfield	KY	(1919–2017, 873-255-32)
871	Massillon	OH	(1894–2017, 871-290-36)

Compiled by the National Federation of State High School Associations (http://www.nfhs.org).

Highest School All-Time Winning Percentages
Through 2017 season…minimum .695 & 500 games played…percentages are rounded to nearest thousandth

Rank and School	Winning Pct.	Overall W-L-T Record	Program Years
1. Cincinnati Wyoming	0.761	688-200-48	1931–2017
2. Newark Catholic	0.749	512-170-4	1958–2017
3. Massillon Washington	0.743	871-290-36	1891–2017
4. Wheelersburg	0.739	498-174-6	1956–2017
5. Youngstown Cardinal Mooney	0.734	487-173-10	1956–2017
6. Upper Arlington	0.725	636-236-18	1926–2017
7. Marion Pleasant	0.719	418-160-11	1962–2017
8. Kettering Archbishop Alter	0.715	419-167-0	1964–2017
9. Steubenville	0.711	806-317-34	1900–2017
10. Avon Lake	0.707	521-211-16	1939–2017
11. Columbus St. Francis DeSales	0.704	436-182-4	1962–2017
12. Mogadore	0.702	662-275-22	1916–2017
13. Convington	0.7	500-211-13	1947–2017
14. Akron Manchester	0.699	532-228-3	1942–2017
15. Canton McKinley	0.695	828-352-42	1894–2017

Source: Ohio High School Athletic Association (http://ohsaa.org)

Ohio's Oldest High School Football Rivalries

Year Started	Rival Schools	# of Games Played
1878	Cincinnati Hughes, Cincinnati Woodward	119
1894	Canton McKinley, Massillon Washington	123
1895	Cincinnati Hughes, Cincinnati Walnut Hills	91

Year Started	Rival Schools	# of Games Played
1896	Dover, New Philadelphia	111
1899	Piqua, Troy	130

As an interesting aside, the National High School Football Records Book has certified that the "All-Time Longest High School Football Rivalry (In Terms of Games)" is Honolulu Kamehameha against Honolulu Punahou at 186 games between 1903 and 2017.

I have spoken to several fans, players and coaches from states around the country who are very familiar with high school football in Ohio and some of the other major states in the nation that have notable high school football reputations. The number one observation I hear is that Ohio has a very high passion for the game, more so than most others, save maybe Texas. Texas seems to be on par with Ohio in its unwavering and devoted loyalty to the game.

Joe Gutilla, the athletic director and head football coach at Cardinal Stritch High School in Oregon, Ohio, told me, "In California [Coach Gutilla played his high school football in California], the state is so big the passion for high school football depends upon which part of the state you're in. Probably the two-best areas are the Southern California [Orange County/San Diego Area/Canyons] and Central Valley [Fresno/Bakersfield] sections. The Sac-Joaquin [Sacramento/Stockton] is also pretty passionate." He went on to say:

Other than passion for the game, California high school football is much faster than high school football in Ohio (especially in the offensive and defensive lines); however, Ohio high school football seems to play a much more physical game than they do in California.

While both states seem to crank out close to the same number of Division I football players each year, I think kids in California have more of an opportunity to continue playing college football than kids in Ohio because of the highly competitive junior college system in California. You only have to be a graduate of a high school in California to enter and be eligible to play football at a CA junior college, and (probably more importantly in these tough economic times) a full semester at a California junior college costs between $500 and $1,000.

Coach Gutilla makes some good observations. I concur that the passion for Ohio high school football and high school sports in general is extremely high and easy to verify by merely looking at game attendance each Friday night, the news coverage given to each game and the number of schools playing football. It's big! And Ohio players do have some pretty good opportunities to play college ball in state and those bordering Ohio due mainly to the huge number of small colleges in the region. True, most of the opportunities are not Division I ball, but where there is a will to play, there is a way.

Jeremy McGrail of Texas, who runs www.5ATexasFootball.com, noted that comparison of that state's high school football programs to others many times comes down to how many guys went to Division I schools and on to the pros, how much individual talent did they produce, how many championships did they get and so on. He told me, "In Texas, football is not some 'one off' that simply comes and goes with the season. That is much too narrow a scope. Texas high school football is ingrained into the fabric of thousands of communities statewide." Well said, Jeremy! Same here!

He added, "Football is a year-round commitment in Texas for players, coaches and communities alike. There is no such thing as an 'off season.'" He told me that he had lived in five states and had seen games in person or had game tapes of games from eight different states, and he noted that the community involvement in high school in Texas is "unlike anything I have seen." He said, "The only other place I know of that can claim something similar is Ohio, but that's obviously on a much smaller scale than Texas given the geographical differences."

Jeremy stated that public and private schools have long been separated in competition and that Texas does not have the "factories" that have come to dominate in other states. He told me that transfer rules are tightly governed by the University Interscholastic League (UIL), the Texas high school athletic governing body, so there aren't multiple transfers to power programs, a situation not enforced in many states.

The lack of separation between public and private high school sports programs is an old issue here in Ohio. In the 1960s, there were complaints that some of the private schools from the bigger cities were nothing but "recruiting factories," creating an unfair advantage over the public school programs. Today the debate rages on.

Jeremy feels that the talent level in Texas is well distributed and becoming more so as Division I prospects are being found in all corners of the state and not just in the metropolitan areas of Dallas/Fort Worth, Houston, Austin and San Antonio. He said that the rural areas of Texas have become very fertile recruiting grounds for schools around the nation and that eleven different programs in the Texas 5A division have won state championships in the 2000–2009 span. He concluded with the point, one with which I concur, that in looking at the *USA Today* Top 25, it seems like the same programs or groups of programs from each state are regularly featured. In Texas, only recently did one school win three consecutive championships, each season going undefeated, that being Southlake Carroll from 2004 to 2006. That had never happened before in Texas.

ATTENDANCE

Simply put: Ohioans love going to football games. In the 1942 season just after Massillon had whipped Steubenville, 33–13, in front of 18,400 fans for its forty-eighth straight victory, its five-game attendance total stood at 74,000 people, for an average of 16,500 per game. At the time, Massillon only had 26,000 residents, and were hoping to better the previous year's mark of 151,500 fans for a ten-game schedule. Their average game attendance average was better than 95 percent of the nation's colleges and universities at that point in the season, being only 1,250 persons behind LSU and only 250 persons back of Stanford per game! Imagine that!

In 1940, Paul Brown's last season coaching Massillon, the team drew 187,000 people. Attendance figures like this are still with us at schools in Cleveland, Massillon, Canton and Cincinnati. Some Ohio schools playing one-off games against prominent teams from other states routinely draw big numbers in the range of 20,000 to 30,000. Combined attendance for all seven 2017 Ohio state finals was 61,312. This was the first time since 2013 that the games were hosted in Stark County and the first time all seven class championships were played at the renovated Tom Benson Hall of Fame Stadium (before that it was known as Fawcett Stadium). It's a gorgeous place to play and home to high school, college and professional games.

Do It Our Way

Witness some of these stories of select Ohio high school football programs to further understand the passion in the Buckeye state for our game. The Martins Ferry football program was profiled in the November 2, 1962 issue of *Life*, written by John R. McDermott. Head Coach Bob Wion was quoted as saying at a Booster Club meeting, "So you see, my job is not really to win football games. It's to make better citizens out of each and every one of your boys. If we don't win a game, all season—and still accomplish that—I'll be happy." The article noted the chilly stillness after that comment, and then an obscenity broke the silence, followed by laughter. Coach Wion, embarrassed, sat down. Later, a Booster Club member saddled up to him and said, "Don't feel too bad about what happened, Coach. Remember one thing—we're with you—win or tie." A fan was quoted as saying, "A losing coach does not walk the street the next day. He walks down the alleys." For these mill towns along the Ohio River, winning was all that mattered.

Players in Martins Ferry embraced the strict discipline that was part of the program, the result of which was that delinquency in the town was almost nonexistent. Dropouts were down—only four that year. Everyone from parents to teachers took an active part in overseeing the players' lives, making sure they studied and stayed on the straight and narrow. The players were also empowered to do a lot of self-policing, holding trials for infractions, like when a guy missed the 10:00 p.m. curfew. This attention paid off in developing better players and winning teams and created an opportunity for a young boy to escape the town and achieve something grander than working in a mill, which a lot of parents wanted their boys not to do. The article stated that in the year before, four players from Martins Ferry had moved on to play big-time football at West Virginia, Tennessee, Indiana and the Air Force Academy. Martins Ferry and other mill town schools on both sides of the river along the thirty-five-mile stretch of the state in the Ohio River Valley has long been a slingshot for these tough kids to escape from the life their rugged parents had endured, at the time having sent more than three hundred kids on to college. Forty-seven of them had gone on to play professional football by then, including Lou Groza from Martins Ferry (Browns) and Nick Skorich from nearby Bellaire (Eagles). A congressman from the area quipped that "half of our area's tourist trade comes from college football scouts."

Coach Wion himself saw some of the more demonstrative passion when a fan was once verbally berating him and one of his players jumped into the stands and punched him. The coach himself got into the violent side when he assaulted a former deputy sheriff who was abusing one of his players. The fight cost the coach a $500 fine and his victim eighteen stitches on the forehead. Described in the article as "Marine drill instructor" like, the respect he got from his players was total.

In Sandusky, the booster club had a reputation for direct involvement in the game and the players' lives and motivation, much like in Martins Ferry. One time, when boosters did not think the players were tough enough, they sent some live chickens to the locker room just before halftime, the message being conveyed that the guys were chicken and had to play harder. On another occasion, they sent a dress to the star of the team at halftime because they thought he was acting like a prima donna. The guys apparently got the message each time.

Sandusky has a tradition of excellence going back more than one hundred years, and the history of a program can be an effective tool in turning out great players and successful teams who win championships. In a set of guidelines and rules that the program gave its players titled *Sandusky High School Football Handbook*, the author wrote:

> *All of the great football players in the history of Sandusky High School have set up these training rules. They were willing to go "all out" for forty-eight minutes every game. They were able to do so because of superb conditioning. Are you capable of stepping into their shoes? No matter how big you are, or how fast you are, nothing will give you the confidence of filling their shoes as that thrill of knowing that you are able to go all out.*

Now, if that paragraph doesn't want to make you jump through a brick wall, do a five-mile or run the stadium stairs holding a twenty-five-pound barbell plate in front of you, well, I guess nothing will then. But this was typical of the motivation used by Ohio programs and coaches.

In Troy, they had a "feeder" system in which football began in the fifth and sixth grades, playing touch football only. Tackling started in seventh grade. Any kid who went out for football stayed, but if he quit, he was not allowed back on the team. This concept was based on military unit loyalty, a devotion to one's comrades, guys with whom you shared hardships. I remember my senior year, we had a pretty good guy, athletically above average, who played running back and defensive back. He missed two or so weeks of two-a-days and then came out for the team. Our coaches asked the seniors if we wanted to have him on the team. We said no, basically because he had not shown devotion to the team by skipping the hardest part of the season. It was a wise move by our coach to empower us, and we all learned from it. The Troy model, therefore, ensured a consistent number of players from year to year.

At Roger Bacon High School in Cincinnati, the staff published a handbook for players years ago that laid out expectations clearly for those boys contemplating playing football. Bron Bacevicha—a man with a stellar coaching reputation who coached the Spartans from 1954 to 1973 and ended his career there with a 150-40-7 record for a 76 percent winning percentage—wrote in his tome *Varsity Football—Basic Information*:

> *Roger Bacon Football—The basis of our football is SPEED, AGILITY, GUTS, BRAINS AND 100%-PLUS EFFORT, both on and off the field. Our teams are noted for TOP CONDITION during the entire game, for vicious aggressiveness, for explosive spirit. This brand of football has made Roger Bacon known throughout the state. It has been made possible by the many great, wonderful players who have played before. This heritage is YOUR challenge to equal or SURPASS THE RECORDS of the past.*
>
> *Training Rules—You cannot play championship football without making sacrifices. Abiding by the Spartan code is just one of those. Our TRAINING RULES are based on just plain, COMMON SENSE. You will be asked to do things that are good for you. You will not be asked to make any sacrifice your coach won't make.*
>
> *Where Will You Play? At Roger Bacon, we only recognize football players. EITHER YOU ARE OR YOU'RE NOT. If you ARE a football player, you will always want to play where you will do the team the most good. Whatever may be your lot, be the BEST. Never ALIBI. Never COMPLAIN. When you want something better—WORK HARDER.*
>
> *Quitting—No one compels you to play. It is an HONOR to play on a school team, a greater honor to play on a ROGER BACON TEAM. If you CHOOSE to play football, go through with it, DON'T BE A QUITTER.*

The Niles McKinley program of this era also used psychological tricks to stimulate its players to a higher degree of accomplishment. Coach Tony Mason, an Ohio High School Hall of Fame coach (2002) and a former coach at the University of Cincinnati and the University of Arizona, did some things during his tenure as the Red Dragons coach that helped his team focus and dedicate themselves to achieve more than they ever realized. They came to be called "Masonisms."

Coach Mason liked to use key words to convey what he wanted. He wouldn't give a simple command, like "tackle him," but would add "viciousness" in the sentence, such as, "hit through him with viciousness." Coach Mason compiled these terms to use throughout the program, and they included phrases like "certainty of goal," "exactness," "clear cut of aims" and "forced silence." The devil is in the details, they say, and to constantly impart to his players that every little thing matters, he made them better. He painted a red line at the edge of the practice field between the field and the locker room. His schedule for practice and activities was usually expressed in half-minute increments because he believed the guys would remember that time better than just a whole number, such as practice starting at 3:14½ p.m. instead of 3:15 pm. If the players were not across the red line by 3:14½ p.m., they were not allowed to practice that day. This was another tactic that instilled pride and unity into the group.

The Niles staff told the players that there were no friends on the field and that they were to practice as such, especially in one-to-one drills, to bring out their "ferociousness." Injured players wore a yellowish-brown jersey, and they all strove to get it off as a soon as possible. A boy not wearing one of these specially colored jerseys was ready to "knock and hit."

The Mothers Club in Niles worked with the coaching staff to put on a swimming party called "Farewell to Sweets." Held near the end of July, it was the last time a player ate any sweets, swam, drove a car or dated his girlfriend. Niles players attended an etiquette class to learn how to be proper, use their manners and dance. At the end of the season, the team selects an all-opponent team and invites eleven of them to an all-opponent dance. The players did all the decorating and serving, wearing aprons, and the entire student body and administration was invited.

Because of this, the Niles McKinley Red Dragons have always been in the top echelon of Ohio high school football.

Coaches Grow Here

Ohio has long been a breeding ground for outstanding football coaches at all levels. In addition to the overall football culture described previously, there is the multitude of small and mid-size colleges and universities that dot Ohio, allowing for a lot of players to play after high school and a lot of coaches to coach after graduating. Known as the "Cradle of Coaches," Miami University in Oxford, Ohio, developed a reputation for schooling and cultivating football coaches who go on to lead big Division I and professional teams. The list of those who have either graduated or coached at Miami University is a who's who of football royalty: Woody Hayes, Bo Schembechler, Ara Parseghian, Weeb Ewbank, Paul Brown and Sid Gillman.

In addition, did you notice how many coaches came to coach at Massillon and then went from Massillon to bigger jobs? They all wanted Massillon on their résumé.

In an article published on September 13, 2018, on the MaxPreps website (www.maxpreps.com) and written by Kevin Askeland, the case was presented for the fifty greatest high school football coaches of all time. MaxPreps used a formula that included wins, average wins per year, winning percentage, state titles, national championships and state championship percentage. A coach needed ten years of coaching or 375 wins or at least one national championship for consideration. National championships were those selected by either the National Sports News Service, *USA Today*, the National Prep Poll or MaxPreps. Coaches with a national championship but less than ten years coaching high school football were not considered.

This excellent analysis notes that most of these figures coached during a time when playoffs existed and thus played more games per season. In contrast, Paul Brown at Massillon coached ten games per season. Plus, not taken into consideration was the league play these teams encountered. Some leagues in these states—such as those tough teams that Mater Dei High School in Santa Ana, California, encountered on a weekly basis—should also be in the conversation when doing such lists, but it is difficult to quantify.

In the Top 50, Ohio had the following coaches listed:

No. 6 Chuck Kyle, Cleveland St. Ignatius
Years coached: 35 (1983–2017)
Record: 345-87-1 (.798)

Average wins per year: 9.9
State championships: 11
State championship percentage: .314
National championships: 3

No. 11 Paul Brown, Massillon Washington
Years coached: 11 (1930–40)
Other Teams: Severn (Md.)
Record: 96-9-3 (.903)
Average wins per year: 8.7
State championships: 6
State championship percentage: .545
National championships: 4

No. 16 Gerry Faust, Cincinnati Moeller
Years coached: 19 (1962–80)
Record: 178-23-2 (.882)
Average wins per year: 9.4
State championships: 5
State championship percentage: .263
National championships: 4

No. 28 Chuck Mather, Massillon Washington
Years coached: 14 (1937–41, 1945–53)
Other Teams: Brilliant, Leetonia, Hamilton
Record: 111-18-5 (.847)
Average wins per year: 7.8
State championships: 6
State championship percentage: .429
National championships: 2

No. 42 Leo Strang, Massillon Washington
Years coached: 18 (1946–63)
Other Teams: Caldwell, Upper Sandusky, East Cleveland Shaw
Record: 127-26-1 (.828)
Average wins per year: 7.1
State championships: 3
State championship percentage: .167
National championships: 2

Massillon, which has won more national football titles than any high school, showed strong with three coaches in Brown, Strang and Mather, while Valdosta, Georgia, which has won more games than any high school in the nation, had two with Wright Bazemore and Nick Hyder. Texas has the most coaches on the list with seven. Seventeen coaches were still active when this article was published.

The Future of Ohio High School Football

As noted previously, the economy surrounding a high school program can affect its success. Marion, Ohio, my hometown and home to two state champion football schools, suffered a decline beginning in the early 1970s. Businesses were closed or consolidated and people laid off, and the available pool of boys for both city schools declined. Like many towns where this was happening, people moved to other cities following the jobs. In some cases, what once was would never be again. Marion Catholic, a two-time state champion, had to close its doors a few years ago due to declining attendance.

To give more schools a chance to play and experience the camaraderie of football, the state went to a class system in the '60s based on school size. This was the same for most states. Out west, many states had to go to six- or seven-man football because of the dearth of available kids and lack of budget. In Ohio, pay-to-play solutions came into vogue, with the parents paying anywhere from $200 to $300 or more per season for their kids to participate in football. Both macro- and microeconomic factors play a role. Only in the most economically stable communities today will teams be able to sustain their programs tomorrow. But the biggest potential impact to the future of football in Ohio and elsewhere depends primarily on safety.

Risks

The risk of playing football has always been high. The numbers of deaths of players have ebbed and flowed since the game started, sparking calls for reform and/or elimination of the sport altogether. President

Theodore Roosevelt personally intervened in 1905 by calling for safety reforms. In a *USA Today* article dated October 28, 2015, sports columnist Christine Brennan asked the question, "Would football stand a chance if invented today?" Indeed, would anybody approve funding for a sport where there is a chance for the death of a teenager? Or possibly a chance of a permanent injury? If these risks were not enough, the powers to be would not approve football today because of the liability issues associated with it. At the time Brennan wrote this article in 2015, there had been seven football-related deaths in seven weeks. There were also then about 1.1 million kids playing high school football and an estimated 3 million playing youth football. It did not look like it was going away, but there is a data-confirmed trend today of burgeoning athletes going with less violent sports. And let no one say different: football is all about knocking the other guy on his butt.

So, football is here to stay for the foreseeable future, but this dark specter remains a constant. Limiting tackling drills and hitting (like the Oklahoma Drill) in practice along with learning proper technique, creating better helmets, staying hydrated, having doctors and trained EMTs close by, changing rules to ensure safety and stressing overall sportsmanship are keys to keeping the game from becoming a cautionary tale rather than a celebration of athleticism. Telehealth, the use of apps and mobile technology to instantly link to healthcare professionals to patients, could also be useful to those schools that cannot afford sideline doctors. All of this must be there in some form or another to keep the players safe.

I do not remember hearing the word *concussion* in high school, just the phrase "getting your bell rung." Fortunately, we had no major injuries on our team, and the whole aspect of being incapacitated or even dying was never mentioned. If it was, I was not listening. To be honest, it was too much fun, and I was part of something I had always wanted to do. Let's hope all these efforts make it safe for the generations to come.

THOSE WERE GOOD TIMES...

My mom told me before my sophomore year at Marion Harding to enjoy my next three years of high school (no middle school back then), as they would be the best time of my life. She was right. Those years were pretty much carefree. We worried only the little worries that high school kids did and not the bigger ones that were to come: of jobs, finances, health and having kids of your own.

I played football from the grade-school flag game sponsored by the YMCA on to tackle football from seventh grade forward and never had more fun in my life. At my junior high school, we won the city championship, and I remember it was a rainy, muddy day. In the euphoria of the victory, we trotted from the high school back to our junior high and did belly slides on the wet, cold grass surrounding it. Passersby in cars stared at us in wonderment.

I think today of all the guys I played against and wonder what happened to them—all these guys from Cleveland, Columbus, Elyria, Mansfield, Fremont, Lorain and Sandusky. Do they now feel about their high school playing days as I, or do they harbor different memories? I hope not; I hope it was fun for them too.

They say the older one gets, the better they used to be. Today, I like to think the short pass I caught for 10 yards from our quarterback Frank Gifford really went for 45 yards; I scored the winning touchdown at Homecoming, busting through ten tacklers; and I kissed the prettiest cheerleader in the endzone. None of it happened literally, but bits and pieces over many games add up to my fable ringing slightly true—just not all at once! I think that is the way a lot of us my age who played high school football years ago think. But those old game films (evidence exists!) tell a different story, and that's why most of us prefer our memories. It is a lot more fun to have a noisy party with my former teammates eating wings with three to four pitchers of beer at the table.

A lot of former players I speak to today remember certain guys who went on to become stars. I sure do. I remember Scott May, Elmer Lippert and Mark Deming from Sandusky; Bubba Petty from Mansfield Senior; Rob Lytle from Fremont; Kurt Schumacher from Lorain Admiral King; and Rick Middleton from Delaware Hayes. All these guys I had the good fortune to play against and watch as some went on to enjoy stellar college and, in some cases, professional careers. I feel so lucky to have met those kids and have fond memories of them. At a track meet up at Sandusky, both Mark Deming and Scott May, huge stars, gave me some advice on how to throw the discus better—tips I immediately used and by which increased my throws considerably. I was amazed and wondered a few things: why didn't my coach teach me that stuff, and why did these guys do so? Regarding my coach, he was a good guy, but I am not sure about his knowledge of the discus, having been a runner and not a weight man. From Deming and May, I saw and learned about having confidence both in one's character and skills to give back.

I don't have many bad memories of playing football, and those I do have are mainly those of dirty play. I remember vividly one guy I had just blocked kicked me in the stomach as I was getting off the ground. The amazing thing about such an act was that we were in the open field about twenty yards from the ball. I got up and shoved him hard in the chest, and the guy just laughed. Luckily the ref saw it, and we got a big chunk of yardage from the resultant penalty—stupid move on his part, and I wonder today if he thinks of it or even remembers it.

There are two other things I remember about Ohio high school football when I was growing up and then playing the game. One was the hoopla surrounding the games and the seasons. I loved the stadium lights, the marching band and our cheerleaders. Naturally, I thought our stadium the best around and the band and cheerleaders the greatest in the world—my opinion of all of those having not changed in forty-seven years. The dances after the games; the pep rallies and the bonfires; the intensity of our coaches and the energy of the fans, and finally, coming out of the locker room after a hard-fought game, seeing your date or your parents or the booster club, all wanting to say something to you, sometimes stumbling over it or sometimes just giving you an encouraging touch or nod to let you know it was all right—life would go on. Images linger in my mind of those moments and will never leave.

I watch high school football today and wonder how I would compare on the field to these kids today (they are much bigger and faster than we were). It's a silly wonder, as you cannot compare. But for a kid who played high school football, you seem to constantly measure the performance you see on the field against your own past performance or of those you played against. I find myself many times saying, "Yeah, that kid is good, but there was a kid on Findlay's team in 1970 who would eat him alive if they had played against each other." You just find it hard to admit that you weren't as good then as the kids are today. I will tell you, though, I think the amount of football that is now televised helps young players. To watch games today and see and hear coaches and analysts explain things is great, and it is something I feel we who played back then would have helped us become better players.

With age comes some fun at remembering those things you think you did well and kind of blurring the images of those things you messed up, like dropping a pass or fumbling the ball, both things I did (just one of each, thank God!) and cringe now at the detail I remember of doing both—amazing detail, I should say. I remember scoring touchdowns and conversions, and the main thing I remember of those was the joy that came with them. I don't remember too much detail about those plays (the good things happened quickly—the mistakes seem to have happened in slow motion), just my teammates patting me on the butt and saying "Nice job" and wondering what my mom would think of me. Those were good thoughts. I didn't think of personal statistics or a college career but did get excited at seeing my name in the paper on Saturdays. We had a cable television station in town, and I appeared on there as a Player of the Week twice. That was cool! But nothing too complex—just enjoying life, which meant my family, school friends and football. High school sports, especially football, brought the world together for me and many others.

ABOUT THE AUTHOR

Tim Raab grew up in Marion, Ohio, and played high school football for Marion Harding High School, graduating in 1971. He worked in corporate America for more than forty years, mostly in information technology, and has authored articles on technical subjects for periodicals and websites. He has written numerous articles on rock-and-roll for www.rebeatmag.com. He lives in Powell, Ohio, with his family and three cats.

Visit us at
www.historypress.com